PUBLICITY ON STEROIDS

PUBLICITY ON STEROIDS

How to Launch and Maximize
a Dynamic Publicity Campaign

Frēda Drake

ABOOKS
Alive Book Publishing

Additional copies may be ordered from the publisher for
educational, business, promotional or premium use.
For information, contact ALIVE Book Publishing at:
alivebookpublishing.com, or call (925) 837-7303.

Book Design by Alex Johnson

ISBN 13
978-1-63132-156-6

Library of Congress Control Number: 2021923673

Library of Congress Cataloging-in-Publication Data
is available upon request.

First Edition

Published in the United States of America by
ALIVE Book Publishing
an imprint of Advanced Publishing LLC
3200 A Danville Blvd., Suite 204, Alamo, California 94507
alivebookpublishing.com

PRINTED IN THE UNITED STATES OF AMERICA

10 9 8 7 6 5 4 3 2 1

SPECIAL THANKS

Thank you to Percival Davis, for being both a great father and an inspirational author. He taught me how to read, and then how to write compellingly. He also taught me how to think critically and state my case carefully. I also inherited his sense of humor so, if you don't like this book, blame Dad.

A big, loving hug to my daughter, Morgan Moss. She enhances the lives of everyone she knows. Her wonderful fiancé, Roland Singson, knows this and wisely chose her as his life partner.

To my son, Thomas, I send my love. You're missing, but not forgotten.

I am so grateful for my strong support system over the years: Barb Billet, Donna Davis, Cindy & Charles DiMarco, Kristina Evans, Matt Hurst, and Liz & Bud Plotts.

Thank you to Ed DuCoin, CEO of Orpical, for giving me the push and inspiration that I needed to start this book.

Tom Brown (The Tom Brown Show / Rebellion News) has been my encouragement, my confidant, and friend. Hey, Tom. Hey, hey, hey. Hey.

Thank you to my sister-in-law, Ester, who brings us a delicious meal each week so that I can concentrate on other projects. Hugs for my brother, Seth, who blessed us all when he married you.

A "hey girl!" to Maureen Famiano. We were both chosen. We both won.

A big shout-out to my current publicity team: Seth Czerepak, Tom Denham, Miguel Lantigua, David Maas and Dave Purdy.

You are incredible professionals and I'm privileged to work with (and learn from) you. You helped make this book better through your contributions.

I am blessed with many other wonderful friends who believe in me. I'm sorry I can't name every one of you. Thanks to all of you for being there for me, caring about me, and being a phone call away.

I will always be grateful to Eric Johnson, Founder and COO of Alive Media and Publishing Group, for believing in and encouraging me.

Finally, to all my past and present clients: You are the reason I wrote this book, and you may even be in it.

CONTENTS

PREFACE
WHY DID I WRITE THIS?

I've dealt with countless numbers of clients over the years. The biggest complaint they make about other publicity firms is "I had a publicity campaign, but nothing came of it." I would dig into the problem and discover that nothing came of it because they did nothing with it. My clients almost never make that complaint, because I teach them what I'm going to teach you.

My goal is to give you the tools so that you can learn how to create and take full advantage of a publicity campaign, enhanced with marketing and sales. I won't simply teach publicity techniques. I'm going to teach you publicity on steroids.

There are books on publicity. There are books on marketing. There are books on sales. But I've never seen a book about how effective those three are when they're working together synergistically. Frankly, it's long overdue, and you'll see that I'm obviously deeply passionate about all three subjects.

And, although many people in the industry use ghostwriters, I did not use one for this book. I didn't want to go through any filters to connect directly with you. You'll hear, in my voice, some of my wins and some of my raw and painful losses, fantastic examples from my current company (The Reps) as well as experiences from companies I've worked for previously. You'll also hear from members of my own team, as well as industry experts.

YOU DON'T KNOW WHAT YOU DON'T KNOW

Most people, no matter what profession they're in, believe that they understand publicity, marketing and sales.

Often, business owners and authors feel they're qualified to do these things themselves, but they're wrong. Sometimes it's because we professionals make it look easier than it is. Sometimes it's because they had some major wins in their past, and they think they can just do the same thing again. Later I'll give you an illustration of when I once made that mistake, and what the consequences were.

Although the average person understands what a five-star chef does for a living, that doesn't mean they can go into his restaurant's kitchen and easily replicate it.

Experts in every field watch trends and then skillfully apply those ideas to everything they do. Because of this, they know and do certain things, in certain ways, that the average person doesn't know and perhaps has never even realized.

"I DON'T NEED THIS: MY CAMPAIGN IS GOING TO GO VIRAL"

Over the years I've had clients ask me to get them noticed by "social influencers" or to help them "go viral."

One example that comes to mind is when I spoke with a company that felt they had a solid-gold marketing idea to help promote a charitable message.

In a nutshell, they came up with something they felt was entirely unique and fun. They had already decided that a celebrity was sure to sign on as a spokesperson, and that it was going to take off and eclipse the Ice Bucket Challenge, which was trending around that time.

I was given the unenviable task of telling them that this wasn't going to happen overnight.

They were shocked. I'd told them that their underlying motives were fantastic, and I'd applauded their goals. Why was I now telling them that this wasn't going to happen immediately? "Where has your enthusiasm gone?" they asked with a mixture of anger and surprise, like a jilted boyfriend.

I explained my enthusiasm remained the same, but we had to approach this rationally.

Their idea had some problems. Now, that's not a deal-killer! But the massive obstacle I faced was their demand that we make it go viral, when there is really no such thing as a viral campaign.

Yes, you read that right.

Let me repeat it.

There is really no such thing as viral marketing.

Trust me: I was surprised when I finally realized this. I spent years in marketing and publicity, wondering why I could never quite make many of my fantastic ideas go viral. I was always kicking myself all over the place, studying stats, wondering why these campaigns were almost always good, but not great.

What I was missing was perspective.

But that's where Derek Thompson comes in.

Derek Thompson is a senior editor at *The Atlantic* and a weekly news analyst for NPR's "Here and Now." He's a triple threat, with a triple major in journalism, political science, and legal studies. He has appeared on *Forbes'* "30 Under 30" list and *Time's* "140 Best Twitter Feeds."

One of his most recent books is *Hit Makers: The Science of Popularity in an Age of Distraction*. The book addresses common misconceptions about marketing and publicity, and gives incredible insights for anyone interested in either.

In answer to the question "Do ideas really go viral?" Thompson writes:

The answer appears to be a simple no. In 2012, several researchers from Yahoo studied the spread of millions of online messages on Twitter. More than 90 percent of the messages didn't diffuse at all. A tiny percentage, about 1 percent, was shared more than seven times. But nothing really went fully viral—not even the most popular shared messages. The vast majority of the news that people see on Twitter—around 95 percent—comes directly from its original source or from one degree of separation.

His book cites numerous studies, and deals with what we often perceive as a "lucky" break which, in reality, took time and persistence in the face of almost sure defeat.

In other words, if something comes across your radar today, it was most likely at least months, if not years, in the making. And this is what I had to tell my potential clients: There are no easy fixes, no easy answers, and no shortcuts.

Viral marketing is a myth we'd love to believe in, just like we'd like to believe something as simple as vinegar can cure all ills. It makes the complex understandable and achievable!

But now that I've popped that balloon, let me offer you some hope.

The good news is that with hard work, persistence, and investment, you stand an excellent chance of being noticed and eventually having your campaign take off and 'go viral.' This book has been written to help you achieve that goal.

OLD PUBLICITY TECHNIQUES DON'T WORK

Periodically someone will call me and insist that they want a press release. They're always shocked when I tell them that they probably don't want that. "I *know* what I want," they say. "Write up a press release and then send it out."

Right. So it can end up in an online graveyard where other

press releases go to rot. Press releases rarely work, unless they're from a major organization.

For example, if Nike puts out a press release about their latest athletic shoe, people will pay attention. But if Joe Smith has cobbled together what he believes to be a groundbreaking design in athletic sandals, his press release will be ignored. People have no idea who Joe is, or why they should care about his particular invention.

Press releases are mostly a thing of the past, because they get drowned in the noise from every other individual or company that is looking for recognition. What works? Stick with me and I'll tell you.

SOMETIMES MARKETING PRACTICES
ARE OUT OF TOUCH BY DECADES

I once worked for an elderly surgeon. As many medical workers will tell you, surgeons often have a God complex (they believe that they know everything and can do anything). Of course there are exceptions (I have some good friends who are medical doctors) but he wasn't that exception!

During my career there, he would give me various assignments, such as writing television commercials, ad copy, press releases, or graphic designs. I would put a great deal of effort into each project, only to have him slash through it like a wilderness explorer ploughing through underbrush. Suddenly hours of work and beautiful copy were lying at his fingertips, maimed. He would inevitably try to mold what I'd produced into his ideas of what a successful 1970s marketing campaign should look like, because that's when he was in his formative years. The problem was that it was forty years out of date.

The very last project I worked on was the weirdest brochure I'd ever created. "I want you," he declared, "to take all our reviews on Facebook and put them into a beautiful brochure made of thick cotton cardstock. And I want it to look just like Facebook."

Er, what? I was puzzled. So I tried to, once again, explain what social media was and why it would be redundant and unnecessary. Additionally, I added, the project might violate copyright law.

"I don't care," he said. "Just do it." So I did, chafing at the ridiculousness of it all. I finished it the day I gave my notice. I was frustrated by the fact that I was never listened to, and my advice wasn't valued.

SALES TACTICS CHANGE MORE THAN YOU MIGHT REALIZE

My first jobs, as a teenager, were in sales. Later I was a manager overseeing teams of up to forty salespeople. Tiring of sales, I evolved into a marketing director and local publicist, and eventually I became a national publicist.

Over those years, I've seen that the most successful salespeople do not operate in a vacuum. They need publicity and marketing support, which will channel warm leads to them. Then it's their responsibility to turn those leads into paying customers. If they're good at what they do, everyone wins.

And yet, I've seen countless business owners who think they can tell their team how to sell, while, at the same time, not supplying them with any of these tools.

"Here," a business owner said to me once. "Read the script exactly like this. No exceptions."

I read over the script, which had the finesse of a telemarketing pitch. The problem was that it was for a high-end, expensive product.

"Er," I began. "Do the salespeople have to say this exactly?"

"Yes," said the owner, firmly. "Exactly like this."

"But this isn't really geared to the target audience…" I began.

"Look. I was in sales thirty years ago. I know how it works.

This will work just fine," the owner declared.

Most obviously it didn't. And instead of ever rethinking this, he just turned his salesforce into a churn-and-burn operation. The script didn't work, he was too cheap to do a good marketing or publicity campaign, but it was always someone else's fault.

WE ALL HAVE BLIND SPOTS

What do these examples have in common? They show that everyone has blind spots. I have them. You have them. The average person has them. And I've found that this is especially true in publicity, marketing and sales. I've come to believe it's because these three professions aren't properly seen for what they are.

All three appear to be deceptively simple. Why? Because the average person will read a book on publicity, see an article on marketing, or attend a Tony Robbins seminar and get fired up, and think that's all they need.

Many people fail to see the intrinsic artistry in these professions. The best talent in these fields are all artisans: graphics designers, wordsmiths, and silver-tongued communicators who can all adapt to continual change. And that is why I've always loved these three fields. They're a beautiful mix of clever talent and psychology. Furthermore, because the fields are ever-changing, they're never boring.

I KIND OF LIED TO YOU

The first thing you read was "Why Did I Write This?" and really, it was incomplete. I do have another motive.

I also want to persuade you to be more open-minded as you go along that path. You may choose to use the tools I'm giving you to have a successful publicity campaign, or you may choose to use this book as a guide when you select someone else to do it.

LEAD, FOLLOW, AND GET OUT OF THE WAY

You've often heard that old chestnut: Lead, follow, *or* get out of the way. But a successful leader leads sometimes, follows sometimes, and gets out of the way when she should.

As Ronald Reagan once said, "Trust but verify." And I would expect nothing less of you. I'll help you figure out how to trust when trust is deserved, so that you can lead, follow, *and* get out of the way when it's appropriate.

WHAT COMES NEXT?

I'm going to discuss everything in it's order of importance. That means we'll chat about publicity, then marketing, and finally we'll talk about sales.

"Whoa," you might say. "Sales is *last?* I mean, c'mon! There are *tons* of sales books out there! Sales is super important!"

Well, yes! Yes, it is. And because that topic has been covered effectively and powerfully by other authors, I'll recommend books to help you on that particular journey. What I'm going to cover are the points that I rarely see discussed anywhere else.

You see, sales don't happen in a vacuum. In fact, if you're not publicizing and marketing, your salespeople have to do that. And they're not specialists in those areas, so they're bound to be less effective. But if the client is already interested, due to publicity and/or marketing, the salesperson can do what she does best: Sell.

CHAPTER 1

PUBLICITY BASICS

Think publicity has to be expensive, flashy and altogether big-budget? Think again. Today, publicity is about grabbing the attention of your target audience through free (or almost free) publicity rather than simply spending money on advertising.

Even if your company is going through a difficult time or needs an image overhaul, publicity can do wonders for improving its image and increasing sales. So, make publicity your priority. If you're in business, publicity isn't a luxury; it's an imperative. It's the lifeblood of any organization that wants to stay competitive and grow in today's economy. That means the best publicity is ongoing publicity.

Say you open a newspaper today, or go online, as most of us do every morning. And when you do, you'll click on that article you want to read. As you scan that article, you see a quote from a key opinion leader. Often that quote that she makes can be very compelling. In fact, you might share that article! And you can be sure that she didn't appear in that article by accident. That type of media exposure is known as "earned media." When it comes to publicity, you can't buy your way into a publication. You earn it through your credentials.

Readers that might ignore an ad will take earned media exposure far more seriously. Moz.com reports, "There are...specific content types that do have a strong positive correlation of shares and links. This includes research backed content and opinion forming journalism. We found these content formats achieve both higher shares and significantly more links."

Therefore, your chances of being seen are far better with a quality, ongoing publicity campaign. Even marketing firms use publicity because they understand the value of the investment.

WHAT IS PUBLICITY?

Despite an increasing amount of public information about publicity, many small business owners are still unfamiliar with it.

Publicity is different from paid advertising or marketing: *It is not intended to generate immediate sales, but rather to create ongoing positive exposure for you and/or your company.*

For example, if you have ever been interviewed by a local newspaper, you know that article is only a part of the process. You can't rely on one interview to create a message that should be continually reinforced.

Publicity involves getting your business' name and message in front of people who could potentially hire you or buy from you in the future. It can be particularly beneficial to new small businesses that are trying to make their mark in their area, whether it's a geographical area or a competitive marketplace.

Publicity is about earning your way into media that can't be bought or paid for.

Peter Drucker once said, "Business has only two basic functions: innovation and marketing." He should have added one more thing: Publicity. Companies that engage in all three religiously include Apple, Nike, and some companies that are not always seen as true "companies" (but are, nevertheless, highly successful) such as our military.

"Our military?" you may ask in surprise. Yes. Over a couple decades the military went from being perceived as something most young people would avoid to something that helps pay for college, conveys status, and builds a solid work ethic. Their publicity campaigns have made it possible for the military to continue without a draft, and it certainly makes their recruiters' jobs easier.

Publicity campaigns don't always show immediate results. But according to CEB, Inc., "Buyers are 57% through the purchasing process *before* they engage sales." That means that what they see *first* makes all the difference.

If you don't have your marketing and public relations outreach in place, you've already lost many of your customers. These titans are the quiet-running gears behind the scenes that keep customers interested and informed.

PUBLICITY AND MARKETING ENHANCE EACH OTHER

I love talking about publicity. Sometimes the biggest mistake someone can make is to ask me about it. I almost immediately launch into an excited burst of information, because I feel it's one of the most interesting issues there is.

I was delighted to speak on the same platform as Steve Forbes a couple of years ago. I've never been more excited and nervous, but it quickly became effortless since I transmitted that excitement to the audience, and they eagerly participated in a series of questions and answers that took us past our deadline.

I began everything by talking about candy.

When I speak in public, I always mention the old Reese's Peanut Butter Cups slogan: *"Two great tastes that taste great together."*

Whether you prefer chocolate or peanut butter, the magic of Reese's is that both flavors are just so complimentary! You need both peanut butter and chocolate to make this American classic, and you also need a good public relations campaign to compliment your marketing efforts.

Perhaps you're thinking, "you're just saying that because you're a publicist."

Well, no doubt we all want to think we're special. But we *know* publicity is special.

Look: How many of us get to have our cake and eat it too? But if you're doing it right, publicity is how you get into earned media. Marketing is media you pay someone to print or display. And marketing materials should be mentioning your publicity wins every time you have one. Publicity proves legitimacy, and it shows everyone that you are a force to be reckoned with. Publicity pays for itself twice.

See? You *can* have your cake (or peanut butter cup) and eat it too.

NATIONAL VS. LOCAL PUBLICITY CAMPAIGNS

There are many misconceptions about national and local publicity campaigns. Both types send newsworthy information to a wide variety of media outlets in print (online or offline), radio or TV.

Over the years, I've encountered many businesses that believe they only want a local publicity campaign. When I hear that, I say, "What if your patients or clients saw you in the *Wall Street Journal*? Would they say 'Oh, forget about that guy. He was only in the *Wall Street Journal*. He never appeared in our local paper.'"

My clients are always surprised by this, and then they universally agree that national press is just as valuable, and sometimes more valuable, than local press.

That doesn't mean that I can get everyone into the *Wall Street Journal*. But you'd be surprised by how many people are still delighted to be quoted in *The Des Moines Register* or the *Dallas Morning News*.

There are some exceptions. Sometimes local publicity is the best option for a business that provides services exclusive to that community. For example, a local restaurant that doesn't want to expand should avoid a national campaign.

My favorite local diner is called Rosie's Restaurant by the locals, even though it's actually named after her husband. She's the face of the restaurant and she is happiest in her element, running to and fro between customer and kitchen, spreading a little gossip and a lot of sunshine. It would be hard to replicate her smile and how she knows almost all of us by name. You can't franchise that, and she never wanted to.

This diner gained its reputation, in part, due to exceptional American food. Rosie has the best chocolate-chip pancakes around and her Southern grits are magical. Although it's right in the middle of a tourist destination, all the regulars are locals.

Rosie's Restaurant would be unable to handle any other customers and they have no great ambitions, so they would *not* be a candidate for a national campaign. Instead, they thrive on a small advertising budget (marketing) and a lot of word of mouth (local publicity).

However, for most businesses, national publicity is almost always the best option. It's where the big kids play for bigger stakes.

A WORD OF WARNING

Although you may want to take advantage of every opportunity you encounter, always be sensitive in both your publicity and marketing outreach.

For example, no one respects someone that tries to make a name for themselves during a tragedy, with some exceptions. If there's a school shooter incident, it's perfectly OK to let the media know that you're a psychologist trained in diagnosing troubled youth (if you can help identify the root of the problem and how to solve it). It's *not* OK to use the tragedy to try to convince people to buy your bulletproof vests.

You also must be careful with timing. I once was about to release a client's article to nationwide media when the tragically mismanaged Afghanistan withdrawal occurred. I held back because, first, it had nothing to contribute to the big story, and two, it would have been lost in the vast amount of media surrounding the terrible event. At worst, it would have clogged up journalists' inboxes when they were absorbed in finding experts to speak about the crisis, and they could have become so annoyed that they blocked us altogether.

CHAPTER 2

WHAT'S YOUR ANGLE?

The media is always looking for interesting, new topics to write about. But don't make the mistake of believing that they won't cover the same old story over and over again. Many times, just like us, they like to fall back on the familiar. So don't be discouraged if your competitor just had a successful run in the press. You can, too!

But most clients have this common misunderstanding: They don't think about *what* would be interesting to the media. They think that the media should simply be interested in them because, in some unique ways, they *are* interesting! But the reality is that you must work harder than that. It's your job to find your message and make it heard.

> **"Scandal, publicity, attention**
> **—what you will—is publicity."** ~ *Oscar Wilde*

This Oscar Wilde quote may be the basis for the old saying that all publicity is good publicity. That is absolutely false.

Over the years I've worked with many clients who are desperate to expunge their bad publicity, whether it's as simple as a bad Google review or as serious as a malpractice suit. That's where a strong publicity team can help. If you flood the market with good publicity, it can water down the bad stuff. When image is important, it's important to project the right image.

In this chapter, we'll take a look at the messages that you're personally transmitting. Then, we'll tackle how to broadcast your company's message.

PERSONAL BRANDING: SNIFF UNDER YOUR PITS

I know of a salesperson with a great body.

"Wait," you might say. "A great body? Shouldn't you be focusing on her other attributes?"

Well, no. Because that's really what she wants us to focus on. Of course, she posts on social media about other things. But every time she makes a major sale, she puts on a tight outfit and gets someone to video her doing a shimmy dance with her clients. Sometimes those clients play along, sometimes they look as comfortable as a mouse at a cat convention. But each time she has the opportunity, she is doing the bump and grind.

I get it. You know the old saying, "Sex sells." But this only works sometimes. And sometimes it turns off the very clients you may be trying to reach. Colleagues may want to avoid the drama by referring potential customers to someone else. And since no one can remain young and sexy forever, it's best to avoid that as your main selling point.

Interestingly, someone challenged this example, saying that it borders on shaming this woman. And yet, I don't believe in turning a blind eye to issues like this. Look: I'm not trying to pick on this woman. In fact, I removed all identifying information. And I've known many women and men that also use similar tactics. Without true examination of such an example, how can we truthfully self-assess? Should we turn a blind eye to others' faults, also overlooking our own?

While some people have told me that they find her antics offensive and unprofessional, others have praised her for it. In this case, she believes her schtick is not impacting her sales, and she's comfortable doing it. Obviously she's not losing sleep over it. But should she?

According to *Quartz in 2017:*

Men, on average, liked the ads with sexual appeal. The women studied did not.
This isn't the first study to arrive at this conclusion. Another meta-analysis in 2015, by researchers at Ohio State University, found brands that used sex in their ads — from sexualized models to showing actual sex organs — were viewed less favorably than brands that ran neutral ads.
And, a 2016 analysis of six years of Super Bowl ads by Ace Metrix — which scores ads based based on how persuasive, likable, informative, attention-grabbing, unique, relevant, watchable, and perception-changing viewers found them, as well as whether the ads made them want to learn more about the brands or buy the products — found that sexy Super Bowl spots scored 9% lower overall than ads without sexy themes.

This, and other similar studies, show that this approach is growingly increasingly ineffective.

There is something to be said for being unique. It's hard to stand out in a crowded field. But too many people stumble across something that works for the moment, and then they allow it to define them for a lifetime. Instead, I would encourage you to find something that sets you apart but won't alienate a portion of the people you are trying to reach.

It pays to do regular audits of yourself because you often will be the only person comfortable enough to be brutally honest with yourself. There's an old Bugs Bunny cartoon where it suddenly hits him that he may not be the most popular rabbit around: He sniffs under his armpits, and says "Do I offend?"

Madonna has been brilliant at redefining herself: Each decade produced a different woman. Now, I'm not suggesting you ditch your jeans for fishnet stockings. But we can learn something here. If we are to be truly successful in life, we need to reexamine the messages we send.

It helps to ask what your goals are.

Do you want to be the top in your field? What image do you want to project? Maybe it's time to buy some suit jackets or trade in the flashy car for something that doesn't make clients wonder if they're paying you too much. What books are you reading that will help you become a better person or better at what you do? What have you been putting off that needs to be done to clear your path to success? Read the New Year/New You articles that pop up in January (our firm really capitalizes on this). You never know what advice will resonate.

But perhaps the best advice is this: Be the person you'd be proud to introduce to anyone, from the bank president to your grandmother... while still being unique, wonderful "you."

EMPHASIZE THE UNIQUE

Sure, you'll sometimes run into the daring promoters who try to sell you on flash and flamboyant behavior. Don't you buy it. People want to do business with individuals and companies they like. Not many people like a diva.

That doesn't mean you shouldn't have a fun persona for you or your company. It does mean that there should always be a line drawn between quirky and downright freaky. An example of this is Richard Branson of Virgin Airlines vs. Howard Hughes. Quirky is the millionaire that insists on wearing an almost identical wardrobe every day. Downright freaky is the millionaire that covers his feet with Kleenex boxes due to his germophobia. Don't be freaky.

With that in mind, you must first figure out what makes you special, so that you can craft successful publicity and marketing campaigns.

I recently saw this company marketing statement:

WHAT MAKES US UNIQUE: We are fanatically passionate about expectations that can be accomplished through clear communication, strategic planning, and a flair for problem solving. We will assess your current situation and find out why you are not getting the results you intended and create a plan-of-action for achieving your specific goals and taking your business to the next level.

Did you fall asleep? Did your mind begin to wander after the first five words? Did you cynically say "Oh suuuuure, like everyone else"?

I'm willing to bet most of you experienced at least one of those reactions.

We've all made similar mistakes. But when your self-summary sounds like a college freshman's paper, it's time to re-evaluate it. This paragraph doesn't make them unique at all. In fact they're boringly similar to every other company in their field. That pitch is as obvious as saying, "we believe in good customer service." Who doesn't?!

When positioning yourself or your company, you must sell the reader on who and what makes you the best choice among your competition. This is called *branding*. Make yourself memorable, and avoid a bunch of dull sentences picked randomly from a sales seminar.

Just before I saw that snore-fest, I read about a company that sells spices. Only spices. And they're absolutely booming.

Why? After all, they're up against major spice distributors like McCormick. When they positioned themselves, they didn't write "We will give you the best spices possible. We'll work hard to make sure every cookie tastes spicy. We have all kinds of varieties and blends." Instead, Calicutt's Spice Company emphasized what made them unique, and it's a huge selling point!

They explained that other spice companies purchase spices from brokers, and spices lose their potency as time passes. Spices can go through many brokers before they end up in a labeled can on your store shelf. That means they're going to naturally be inferior to freshly-sourced spices. And Calicutt's goes directly to the farmers, bypassing the middlemen.

What a differentiator! And it's what makes them unique.

It's why their store continues to thrive on Etsy. Yes: Etsy. It's a small family-owned business and they've carved out a successful niche for themselves because they were able to differentiate Calicutt's from the competition. It was absolutely inspiring! In fact, they've expanded, and have their own website in addition to their Etsy store. Their ability to explain why they were unique made them a desirable supplier.

So...

What makes *you* unique?

STANDING OUT IN THE CROWD

I once worked for a company that specialized in publicity for dentists, and I would often speak at dental conferences. Among other awards, I was given the 2018 Spotlight Award by Dustin Burleson Seminars for my "service and contribution ... and unparalleled coaching to doctors and their employees."

Although we worked with many, many dentists, I can tell you that no two were ever the same. One dentist might be able to talk about the changing role of women in the dental field. Another might want to point out that adults can get braces, too. A third might have been a champion tennis player before he became a full time dentist. These types of distinctions give everyone a unique contribution, even when you're in the same field as your competition. It's why you need to figure out what makes you unique, and capitalize on it.

Sometimes your message doesn't seem to be a good fit for the general media. Perhaps you're a dentist and want to talk about your book, *How to Handle Halitosis*. You want to see it end up in more places than dental trade journals. So, pull back a bit. Can this have a broader perspective?

You can pitch from multiple angles. The dental trade journals and fellow dentists might be excited that you've written a comprehensive guide to the many treatments for bad breath. Perhaps it would be a helpful tool for them, because they could share it with their clients. At the same time, you can put out a pitch to the general media, saying that everyone suffers from this problem some time in their life, and you know how to prevent it.

HELPING OTHERS WHILE HELPING YOURSELF

If you're at a loss to say what makes you unique, consider getting involved in a charity. It's proverbial that *good publicity comes from being good publicly*. If you believe in your organization, let the world know about it by doing your best to share its goodness with others. Publicity is all about helping people connect and feel good about the people and organizations they're engaging with. You don't have to give money to charities. If your budget is tight, give with your time. Offer to help others with your ideas, energy and products. Volunteering your time to a cause you believe in is publicity. In fact, it's probably the most priceless publicity of all.

And don't forget that publicity can even be free publicity for you, personally. If you or your company are doing good things, let others know about what you're up to by connecting with them via social networking sites such as Facebook, Twitter, Instagram, and LinkedIn. TikTok is the newest hot social media platform, which may also work for you. Social media is constantly evolving, so stay up to date. (We'll talk more about this later).

Ultimately, it pays to do the right thing. As Customer Thermometer reports, "13% of consumers would pay 31-50% more for your products or services if they were under the impression that your business is making a positive impact on the world."

WRITE, WRITE, THEN WRITE SOME MORE

You also need to create unique material to give them something to look at. Reporters, talk show hosts, and TV producers want to see what you have to offer, usually before they ever approach you. That means you should be posting regularly to your website's blog, and then sharing it on social media. Don't make the mistake of believing that blogs are out of date. In fact, they are key to driving your website's search engine performance, if you're using the correct verbiage. We'll discuss blogs, and how to utilize them, later in this book.

If you work for a company and don't have your own website, use LinkedIn as your site and publish articles periodically there. Consider writing white papers, or a short guide to something you specialize in and can give away for free. If you collect email addresses in exchange for the giveaway, you can use those addresses in future marketing campaigns. Of course, those marketing campaigns will also require (you guessed it) writing!

CHAPTER 3

WRITE YOUR WAY TO AUTHORITY

U ltimately, the media is interested in you if you can solve problems, and a book is a way to prove that. For example, I signed on a world class epidemiologist just before COVID-19 hit. He had a great book about to come out, warning that it was only a matter of time before the world was hit with another plague like the Spanish Flu, and he had solutions and suggestions. And then COVID-19 appeared. Not only did he end up with an incredible amount of national attention, he also was brought on as an advisor to government at the highest levels.

ONLY WRITE WHAT YOU KNOW

No matter what you write, whether it's books, articles, or white papers, know this: They lend credibility as long as you can truly speak as an authority. You need to stay in your lane. The media wants to know that you are credentialed in what you're speaking about.

For instance, if you wish to write a book about how to create a functional society, you'd better be a sociologist, an anthropologist, or possibly a historian. And if you're a store clerk, you can't write a book about podiatry with any authority, no matter *how* sore your feet get. But, a store clerk most certainly *can* write a book about how to handle customer problems or how to survive under a difficult manager.

I know of a self-styled marketing expert that has written many, many books but they're all out of date and/or about topics he is not an expert in. For instance, many of these books are about medical issues, but he's not a journalist that specializes in researching these topics and interviewing medical professionals. He's not a medical professional, either. He apparently felt that his true worth was in the quantity of books he created, and that content mattered very little. However, anyone looking at this widespread variety would rightly wonder if he could be an expert in anything at all, including marketing.

If you want to be taken seriously, only write about topics in which you are credentialed, or topics where you have first-hand in-depth experience.

IF YOU CAN, TIE YOUR MESSAGE INTO THE NEWS

Sometimes it can seem virtually impossible to find a good angle. I almost turned down a client because she initially told me that she wanted to publicize a coffee table book full of her lovely flower photography. You might think we can publicize everything and anything, but photography is especially challenging to publicize unless we're representing a professional photographer. She wasn't a photographer, she was an attorney. Yet, I took the time to chat with her because she had such an engaging personality.

As we spoke, I discovered that she was the only woman in a small law firm. She wanted to break out and grow, but kept hitting walls. She also confessed that her dream job would be specializing in cannabis law. She had been to many conferences on the legal angles, legalization was blooming *(pun intended)* throughout the United States, and she was excited about the challenges. The state she lived in hadn't made it legal yet, but it was slated for a public vote on the issue. In the meantime, other states were quickly legalizing recreational and medical marijuana.

I'm sure you can imagine how excited I got when I found this out. I talked her into the campaign of her life. Soon she was being interviewed across the nation on major TV and radio shows. *The New York Times* flew a reporter and photographer out to follow her around for two days to write a feature piece. She won accolades and was named one of the top cannabis attorneys in the nation. She left and started her own business. Now she has to turn clients away.

To this day, we still check in on each other. She is a true delight and I just adore her. And there are plans to get that book of flowers finally published. I've encouraged her to include a couple shots of flowering cannabis plants.

WHY WE WRITE AP-STYLE ARTICLES
AND YOU SHOULD, TOO

The better publicity agencies (the ones that are always following the trends) realized long ago that press releases have become mostly ineffective.

"Wait," you say. "You say press releases aren't effective any more. But there are places on the internet where we can still post them, and I even have software with templates for press releases!"

I'm sure you do. I actually have an abacus and calculator in my desk, but I always use the calculator on my phone. Progress marches on.

I can still hear one of my clients, Jim, saying in his thick Brooklyn accent, "OK, genius. So what works?"

I'm glad you asked.

You know about the newspaper layoffs and consolidations. You've seen magazines go out of circulation. You've heard of journalists being laid off. The result is that remaining journalists are overworked and underpaid. Stories that should be covered are being ignored. Now that's bad for the average person that wants to get their story into circulation, but it's great for me because we have the solution for both the publications (online/offline) and those who want to be heard.

We supply the stories.

What we do for our clients is to create articles that we distribute to national print media outlets that are interested in that particular topic.

Many of those articles are published, verbatim. Sometimes a journalist will see the article and say "hey, that's a great idea! I think I'll get in touch with the author and expand on that."

And if you target the article just right, it's discussing a current trend that will also capture the attention of journalists who may be working on a similar story and, voila! Our client is suddenly being quoted alongside other specialists in their field.

TIPS FOR WRITING YOUR ARTICLES OR (WHEN APPROPRIATE) YOUR PRESS RELEASES

The following portion has been written by my colleague, Tom Denham. I'm proud to say I enticed him to come out of retirement to work with us. Tom was a reporter for the daily Tampa Tribune *and an editor of several different community publications. He was also Press Secretary for the Speaker of the House of the Florida legislature and Director of Communications for the Florida Department of Juvenile Justice.*

Journalists consider press releases a necessary evil. They go through them reluctantly, on a regular basis, because reporters are always looking for something to write. If they are having a good week, they don't read submitted articles or press releases. They are working on stories they found themselves by covering their beats, talking to sources and beating the streets. If they are having a bad week and have exhausted every other avenue to find their next story, then they start looking at those articles. No journalist worth his press pass wants to go to a gruff city editor and tell him they have a great story they just found in a press release. Editors want them to find their own stories, but sometimes a supplied article or press release lead is all they've got.

Usually, that article has frequently had a long, difficult journey to get to that inbox. The writer has spent hours researching, editing, bouncing it off co-workers and then editing again before it goes to the client for approval. Then the client frequently sends it to several team members for their input. All these edits then get sent back to the original author, who has to make changes to his masterpiece from people he doesn't even know. Finally it is sent to the journalist where it must clear several hurdles before anything makes it into print.

The First Hurdle:
"Journalists Go Through Press Releases
Like You Go Through Junk Mail"

Think about how you go through your junk mail. You give it a few seconds before you toss it. In a newsroom, the release gets the same treatment—it only has a few seconds to grab the attention of the journalist, otherwise it is quickly thrown away. During that critical few seconds before it is tossed, the reporter will scan the press release looking for answers to these questions:

1) Does it pertain to the reporter's area of coverage? It can be the most interesting piece of prose to ever hit his desk, but if it is something he doesn't cover, he doesn't care. It goes in the trash.

2) Is it timely? Is it about something that is going to happen in the near future? Is it about something that has been in the news recently? Is it local? Is it something that pertains to his specific geographic area? Is it new, unusual or exciting?

Is there something new in the headline or the first paragraph that has piqued his interest? Many successful press releases fall into this category with new products, services or information about technologies not usually known by the general public.

The Second Hurdle: How much editing is required?

No matter how well the piece is written, large newspapers and magazines will typically use the piece as background for a reporter to write his own story. But for the purposes of this book, let's assume the publication doesn't have a huge staff and occasionally the editor uses these stories after he has edited them.

So let's also assume the journalist is interested enough in the first pass that he doesn't immediately toss it. Early in my career when I was an editor for small community publications, we received nothing but press releases. I usually tossed more than half of the ones I received immediately without ever reading more than a paragraph. The releases that were left I would then divide into two stacks: One stack included releases that required extensive editing and one stack that required very little editing.

The stack that needs a lot of editing probably will not be used at all unless the editor is desperate. Usually that type of article or press release will hang around the desk for a day or two and then be tossed when something that requires less editing, or is more interesting, shows up.

The Third Hurdle:
How To Get In The Stack That Will Get Used

When an editor makes a decision on whether an article needs a lot or a little editing, these are the red flags that push it into the less desirable stack that will probably be thrown in the trash:

Too much "fluff." This is the most common error that PR professionals who have never worked in a newsroom make. Adding too many comments about how wonderful the product or service is or that names the company or CEO six times in the first paragraph will doom it to the trash can.

Remember you are not spending all this time and effort on an article just so you can pat yourself on the back. The purpose of the entire exercise is to get it to a mass audience. Many clients believe their product or service is the best thing since sliced bread, but they should save their over-the-top self-congratulations for their advertising budgets.

A public relations professional who can't stand up to the client and tell her that the press release or article needs to tone down the self-promotion will have an easy path to client approval of the release, but it will usually go nowhere in the newsroom.

Spelling or grammar errors: You would be surprised how many press releases and articles are sent out with spelling mistakes most fourth graders would not make.

Poorly organized: The wording is jumbled, with the wrong paragraphs or sentences in the wrong places. It doesn't flow well from one thought to the next.

Too many technical terms: Save the technical jargon for in-house publications because employees know those terms; the general public does not. If the release is about a complicated topic, do your best to explain it in simple terms.

Too many large words, long sentences and big paragraphs: This is usually a big problem for book authors or other white collar professionals who tend to want to write on a more advanced level. However, most target publications are writing to an audience at about the tenth-grade reading level. Paragraphs should be small, sentences should be short, and complicated subjects should be simplified and presented in bite-sized pieces. Just because someone is an authority does not mean they know the best prose to influence a journalist. Most experts should rely on competent public relations counsel, and take their advice.

Too Many Associated Press Style Errors: The Bible in journalism is the *Associated Press Stylebook*. This is available for purchase anywhere that sells books. It is what editors turn to when they wonder if they can substitute FDA for the Food and Drug Administration, Realtor for real estate agent or if it is acceptable to use SUV instead of spelling out sport utility vehicle.

So What Do We Mean When We Say We Will Write Your Pitch in an "Associated Press Style" article?

It means we want it to be the type of copy that a newspaper reporter would write, not the type of copy that has been written to please the boss of the company or the author of the book. When our releases hit an editor's desk, we want the copy to be as smooth as honey. We don't want him to wade through tons of fluff and self-promotion to get to the meat of what would be important to his readers.

When it comes to approving AP style articles or press releases that a publicist has sent you, you should be flexible and remember what an old editor once told me: "No copy is carved in stone."

The pieces that usually get the best coverage are the ones that are written the way most reputable print publications with large audiences write their own copy – succinct, to-the-point and without a lot of hyperbole. The editor makes a few minor changes and moves on. That's our goal, and if you want the biggest audience for your release, it should be your goal as well.

This is the end of Tom's contribution. You may not feel up to learning the AP style of writing, and that's OK. There are other options.

5 REASONS YOU SHOULD CONSIDER LISTICLES

You've read a lot of listicles already, though you may not have realized what they're called. They're articles that have a list of things to note in a particular topic.

Here are five reasons why you should consider writing at least one listicle:

1. They're highly effective for reader click-through because people feel comfortable knowing that there are limitations in the article. "Oh, I can take the time to read *that*," they say to themselves as they open it up.
2. They help keep you organized and focused on your primary message.
3. They create easy bites of info that can later be used in social media messaging.
4. They're less intimidating to write.
5. Everyone's doing it.

See what I did there?

Make sure that your title lists how many bullet points you have in your listicle. It might look something like *"7 Things You Probably Forgot to Tell Your Doctor."*

Now, for listicles to be truly effective, you need to ensure that they're filled with quality data written succinctly. It can be shorter than an editorial, but take the time to give the reader enough helpful information that they won't regret clicking on that link.

CHAPTER 4

WRITE THAT BOOK

Of course, not everyone is born to be a book author. Perhaps you only feel you have a couple of articles or a whitepaper in you. If so, that's OK! It's better than nothing, and it will be material you can use in current and future campaigns. However, we've successfully publicized authors that have produced incredibly short, simple books. No matter what size, books create a stronger awareness of you and your message than simple articles will.

The media is much more likely to pay attention to you if you have a published book.

If you don't know how to write well, or perhaps you simply don't have the time, then consider hiring a ghostwriter. There are ghostwriters available in almost every subject. However, I believe that most ghostwriters, no matter how good they are, tend to produce more muted content. And, if you use a ghostwriter, be prepared to continue using that ghostwriter. James Patterson uses a variety of ghostwriters, which explains why his content is a bit erratic in quality.

Shop around carefully to make sure that the ghostwriter you choose has your same worldview. I know of a case where a ghostwriter was hired to write a book. The problem was that although the ghostwriter specialized in the topic, she was a Millennial and the titular author was a Boomer. The writing styles weren't the same, and their general outlook on life wasn't a good match. In the end, the Millennial had to be replaced with a ghostwriter that was from the same generation as the author, and it finally worked.

If you prefer a one-stop-shop experience, sometimes publishers will charge you a set fee to provide a ghostwriter, publish your book, and do some minor marketing for it. There are also "talk-your-book" hybrid models where you talk with your ghostwriter through a series of recorded interviews, they create the manuscript, and you give it the final seal of approval.

Newest to the game are some interesting new Artificial Intelligence (AI) writing software options. I've played with the best that's currently available, and I can tell you that it still needs some work. But the possibility is exciting, and it may ultimately help people move their books along a bit faster than if they were just sitting in front of a computer screen searching for the right words.

GETTING YOUR BOOK PUBLISHED

Finally! It's done and the manuscript has been read over by people you can trust, facts have been checked, and edits have been made.

You *have* done all that, right?

The reason I ask is that I've seen some terribly written rubbish out there. I've been at business conferences where I've been handed a book and, upon opening it, knew that there was no one in the media that would take that book seriously. You can't just write down anything, slap it between a cover, and call it a book. Even if it's a smaller book, make sure it's a book with high caliber content, proper grammar, and for goodness' sake, please be sparing when you use ellipsis. I get nervous twitches when I see a book littered with them, and they seem to be endemic to books of poor quality.

OK, then. It's time to get published.

BOOK PUBLISHING TODAY:
EVERYTHING YOU NEED TO KNOW

For this portion, I turned to my own publisher, Eric Johnson. He is the founder and owner of ALIVE Media and Book Publishing, The Talk Pod Podcast platform, ALIVE Digital Marketing, and publisher of ALIVE Magazine, the San Francisco Bay Area's eclectic editorial monthly. He has authored hundreds of articles on topics ranging from politics, human behavior and religion, to science and economics, and has contributed business articles for professional trade publications. The following is directly from Eric:

If you're reading this, it's likely you are interested in having a book published or know someone who is—or, you are at least curious about the process. Maybe you've done some research on "self" publishing, but it all seems a bit confusing.

Not to worry. By the time you're finished reading this, you should have a much better understanding as to the process of becoming a published author.

Indeed, that process is far different today than it was just a few years ago. Many of the changes are largely due to ever-evolving technology, as every step in the "author to reader" experience has changed due to those advancements.

Authors of fiction and nonfiction alike have far greater access to information, as well as tools to help in the writing process. Spelling and grammar-check programs are common, for example, as is voice-to-type/dictation software, and the steady growth and sophistication of the internet and search algorithms make research easy. Together, these changes help free the author of some of the labor and mundane aspects traditionally involved in the creative process of writing a book.

How printed books are manufactured today is far different than in years past, as advancements in this aspect of the publishing process continue at an ever-increasing pace. Print-on-demand (POD) technology allows one-off, single-book printing to be accomplished at low cost, within minutes of an order. This means authors and publishers no longer need to order large quantities of books in order to keep unit costs low.

Alongside POD, the process in printing bulk-volume orders has also progressed. Our company, ALIVE Book Publishing, recently placed an order for one of our authors for 5,000 copies of his book. Within five days of the order, all 5,000 copies of his book were en route—printed, bound, boxed, and shipped. Just a few years ago, the printing process alone in this case would have required several weeks at least.

The advent of e-books is, of course, another change. An e-book is simply a device-friendly PDF (Portable Document File) version that one can read on a mobile device or computer. While not appropriate for all books (better than 80% of book-buyers still prefer the tactile experience of printed books), e-books are an attractive alternative for some books, like the "quick read" while you're at the beach on your vacation.

Then, there is marketing and distribution. The gorilla in the room here, of course, is Amazon. This behemoth is doing its best to dominate the entire book universe. Currently, they list about 33 million books for sale. While responsible for the demise of countless small, independent booksellers—a shame, however you look at it—they are not the ultimate authority in books and publishing for many reasons.

In terms of marketing, for example, someone must know about your book before they search for it online. And here, nothing beats good old-fashioned advertising. Traditional advertising methods and human-driven public relations are critical elements in the sales process that Amazon does not and cannot provide. At ALIVE Book Publishing, we have re-published several titles for authors who at first tried Amazon's in-house publishing service. Did you know that most independent, local booksellers won't list or sell books created through Amazon's publishing service? Those authors didn't, either.

The fact is, while Amazon is terrific at warehousing and order fulfillment, when it comes to the more specialized aspects of book publishing, marketing, and sales, their automation-algorithm model is no match for the human touch.

New vs. Old World of Publishing

"I have a manuscript but would NEVER pay to have my book published." Those were the words of a young author in response to my mentioning to him that in addition to publishing this magazine, ALIVE publishes books too, but in most cases the author pays the front-end cost to have their work published.

This viewpoint is a throwback from a bygone era when a handful of large publishing houses served as gatekeepers of the industry. Today, largely due to those technological advancements, this is no longer the case. Independent publishing houses like ALIVE now easily compete with better-known publishers like Random House.

In fact, had that author chosen to submit his manuscript to us at ALIVE Books, assuming we approved his work, in as little as 60-90 days his book would have been in front of the same book buyers throughout the world as the current best-selling authors'.

The Three Paths of Book Publishing

There are three ways to have one's book published: traditional, subsidy, and self-publishing. All have advantages and disadvantages, and the path one takes largely depends upon the reason(s) for wanting to see one's book in print. Some authors simply want to see their work bound in a book format with the intention of sharing it with family and friends; some have a desire to share their story or communicate an idea, and some have commercial success in mind, even if as only a "side benefit" of reason number two.

Path #1: Traditional Publishing

In the past, the traditional route was considered the only path. This is where an author begins the process by sending query letters—essentially a "sales pitch," intended to capture the attention of a literary agent or publisher. The query letter includes a description of the work and the intended audience for it, along with some information about the author (a bio). In this case, if the author's pitch is compelling, they may be afforded an opportunity to have a publisher review the author's manuscript, and if it is "good enough," the publishing house may agree to publish the author's work. If one hopes to have their work considered by publishing houses like Random House or HarperCollins, it is essential that the author be represented by an experienced agent.

Unfortunately for most, this path is a long, unfulfilling process. Few authors "make the cut," as most agents and large publishing companies are so inundated with queries that they reject all submissions they are unable to classify with 100% certainty as "marketable."

The most likely candidates to have their work represented by established agents and considered by "Madison Avenue" publishing houses are celebrities and personalities with well-recognized names (the Clintons, Trumps, Kaepernicks, and Kardashians) or authors who have already demonstrated—through previous subsidy or self-publishing success—that their work sells. Publishing is a business and the days of "speculating" on unknown authors are long gone. The only relevant question publishers ask about an author's manuscript is: "How many books will sell upon release?"

For example, prior to January 2009, *ALIVE Magazine's* fitness columnist was Lorrie Sullenberger, the wife of the now famous pilot, Sully. Before his successful landing in the Hudson River, had Sully approached the major publishing houses with a query letter about his experiences as an airline pilot, it's likely he would have received the typical response—a rejection letter.

However, after a flock of geese collided with his plane and his subsequent artful skill in landing that plane, Sully became an instant celebrity—and a marketable commodity. The result? He was offered a two-book deal by a major publishing house, and eventually a motion picture was produced about the "Miracle on the Hudson."

While traditional publishing provides advantages—namely brand recognition and the ability to have books placed onto the shelves of major book retailers, the profit margin for authors on each book sold can be miniscule. Publishers are betting on mega-sales—preferably millions of books—so they are looking for authors that fall into just a few, select categories. First, they look for proven authors; ones who can reproduce work that will be eagerly snatched-up by fans (such as Grisham, King, Steel, Patterson and Rowling). Next, they are happy to publish the works of someone well known and currently popular: actors, sports stars, and politicians, or anyone making news, like Sully, right after his remarkable landing.

In all these cases, if all goes as hoped, an author might earn thousands or even hundreds of thousands of dollars. And the publishing houses, of course, enjoy significant returns in all these scenarios too.

But what if you are chosen by a major publishing house and your book doesn't sell in the thousands? In that case there are challenges associated with traditional publishing. First off, major publishing houses will remove a book from circulation—designate it as "out of print"—if it fails to sell in significant quantities. Worse still, if a book fails to meet the publisher's sales expectations, they will often demand that any "advances" paid to an author be returned. Ouch!

Unless one has already sold thousands of copies of his work, or has a famous name, most authors might never see their book published. The only reasonable—and wisest—route open to an author is self or subsidy publishing.

Path #2: Self Publishing

It is possible to self-publish your book. The main advantage to self-publishing is that you control 100% of the process. The main disadvantage is… you control 100% of the process!

You will earn the highest margin of profit this way, but that is because you will be doing all the work yourself. The steps involved are numerous, and if your plan is to produce a quality product (your book) that sells well and sells enough copies to be commercially successful, you will need to be an expert in many areas.

Self-publishing means that you will not only write your book, you'll need to edit it, design and create the cover, design and format the interior pages, obtain the necessary ISBN and barcode, file your copyright, and obtain your Library of Congress Control Number. And then you'll need to know where and how to have your book printed.

Then, assuming you want to sell your book with a hope of making money, you'll need to market it. And even though your profit per book can be higher by doing all the work yourself, you still need to sell a lot of books to make very much. To do that, you'll need to know how to make your book available through large online resellers like Amazon and Barnes and Noble, and to thousands of ancillary online wholesalers and retailers. Will you know how and where to make your book available to independent bookstores and libraries throughout the country and worldwide? Will you know how to reformat your book as an e-book and make it available that way in the marketplace, or if it even makes sense to do that? Will you be able to create your own website, promotional materials, and press releases? In short, do you already have the knowledge, technical and artistic skills, connections and resources to truly "publish" and market your book?

Self-publishing is an option if you've written a book. But then again, so is building your own car if you want to travel. However, sometimes just being the driver—or author—alone is a more logical choice.

Path #3: Subsidy Publishing

The final path of publishing is subsidy publishing. Years ago this was considered a second-rate method, supposedly used only by desperate authors whose work was not "good enough" or had been rejected by traditional publishers. It was implied that authors who chose this route were having their work published merely for the sake of "bragging rights," as in, "Hello, my name is Joe Smith, and I am an author."

The fact, however, is that many highly successful writers got their start this way, and in light of the realities of traditional and self-publishing, this is the most logical, effective, and affordable way for any author to have their work published.

To be sure, there are a plethora of subsidy publishing companies to be found online, most offering a menu of various services designed to get your book published. Most have low-cost options to start, but just like in self-publishing, the more they do for you, the more it costs.

One of the major disadvantages of online subsidy publishing companies is their absence of personalized service. Looking at it from their perspective, because they function and compete solely in the very crowded online universe, they have designed their services with that in mind, so they often limit authors to

"A, B or C" cover template options for example, or "Gold, Silver and Platinum" packages, each with narrowly defined options. And in most cases, these services are automated, whereby the author's work is pushed into a pre-existing format—otherwise known as a "cookie cutter process."

Another important consideration with online subsidy or self-publishing companies is their ability—or, more accurately, lack of ability—to market and promote an author's book. While most of these publishers offer a variety of services, they are usually limited to basic things, like providing the author with a stack of postcards, or writing up a press release. Some will even claim to include a website, which is often just a page on the web displaying the author's book, with no functionality included.

The fact is while web-only, cloud-based publishing services can publish an author's book, they are limited in what that entails. You won't be meeting with their art director or designer, for example, to discuss one of the most important marketing elements of any book —the cover. Nor will you be able to select a font style from a vast collection of options for the text of your book. And while these online companies claim to offer marketing services, the fact is, they only offer a thin veneer of "marketing-like" resources at best.

Lastly, there is one other type of service to be aware of: authors who have self-published their own book(s) who now advertise themselves as a "publishing company." While these individuals may have navigated their way through the maze of requirements listed previously in order to get their own book(s) listed on Amazon, this type of service is often akin to someone who wins a case in traffic court marketing themselves as a lawyer. If the first book they published was their own, they may be qualified to guide an author in the self-publishing process, but they are hardly a publishing "company."

Are There Any Other Options?

Does all this sound a bit hopeless? Are you beginning to wonder if there are any viable options available to the author who wants to have their book not just published, but effectively and successfully marketed as well?

Yes, Option #4: Hybrid Book Publishing!

Let's get something out of the way right now: Regardless of the reason an author has for wanting to publish, the only reason any publisher will agree to publish an author's work is if they believe it will be a profitable venture; plainly stated, the goal is to make money—period. Large commercial publishers are banking on a proven track record or an author's celebrity status, while online subsidy publishers offer only a cookie-cutter process and are ill-equipped for more.

After thinking about this dilemma, it occurred to us that with our vast experience in magazine publishing, we could create a kind of "hybrid" publishing company that not only publishes an author's work but does so in ways that meet authors' unique needs and situations.

Enter, ALIVE Book Publishing, where we provide what no online publishing company can—a one-on-one, face-to-face relationship with authors. We consider every publishing project to be a partnership, so we work with our authors and their projects in a hands-on, individual way. One size does not fit all with ALIVE, so we don't have set formulas for the projects we accept. We sometimes invest more in a project than the author because our goal is for the author's book to sell successfully over the long term.

And, ALIVE is uniquely equipped to market and advertise an author's book because we are the only publisher with multi-media publicity, marketing and advertising tools, and the expertise required to put real power into a local, national, and international book launch.

What Can Hybrid Book Publishing Do for the Author?

The typical services we provide for all authors includes personal advice as to the overall concept of the book project; a custom cover design; layout and formatting of the book's interior pages; the determination of the best price for the book; obtaining the required ISBN and barcode for the book; filing for a Library of Congress Control Number; copyright filing; and POD (print on demand) set-up of every book.

We then advertise all our authors' books through Ingram's marketing platforms, highlighting our authors' books to every bookstore and library in the country. This allows book retailers the opportunity to sell our authors' books in their stores. We also list all our authors' books through major online distribution channels like Amazon and Barnes and Noble, Walmart, and Target. as well as throughout an established network of booksellers worldwide. ALIVE Books' direct print book markets include the USA, Canada, the United Kingdom, the European Union, Brazil, Spain, Germany, Italy, Poland, Russia, India, China, Japan, and South Korean. Additionally, ALIVE Books reaches over 100 countries and territories through a vast network of over 40,000 wholesale and retail distribution channels in a relationship with Ingram Books.

We are also able to provide comprehensive editing and formatting in all ebook formats, and we offer a wide variety of marketing and advertising options. We create and run display ads in *ALIVE Magazine*; create professional, fully functional order-fulfillment-capable websites, and can produce professional videos for online and TV, and can conduct local or national publicity campaigns.

Putting It All Together: What Does It All Mean?

While advances in technology have radically changed the publishing landscape to the point where anyone with a computer and a credit card can become a published author, as I noted earlier, this is not going to be enough if an author wants to successfully break into the book market.

If everyone on the planet already knows who you are, you might consider having your book published via the traditional path. If you have all the skills and resources to go it alone, self-publishing may work, and if you're only interested in a short-lived yet expensive ego boost, go ahead and send your manuscript into "the cloud," and hope for the best.

But if your goal is to be serious about your book project and its chances for success, I suggest you elicit the aid of and partnership with a local publishing company that will be as serious and careful about your project as you are.

This is the end of Eric's contribution. I've worked with many other publishers. In fact, both of my parents are published authors. My father was famous in his genre. When I was young, publishing houses would fly him to exciting locales, beg to publish his books, and treat him to everything from fabulous meals to lavish retainers. However, as Eric pointed out, those days are gone. After weighing all the options, I chose Eric and ALIVE to publish my book. Frankly, I like the personal interaction and care that this publishing company puts into their process. And while it's true that you must choose whomever is right for you, I would suggest contacting the team at ALIVE Book Publishing before making a decision. I think you'll find them to be very helpful.

CHAPTER 5

HOW TO GET YOUR MESSAGE INTO THE MEDIA

THE MEDIA'S SOURCE IS OFTEN THE MEDIA

Ever notice how a story can take off and suddenly you hear about it everywhere? When people see a good story, they want to learn more about it.

But to get that story out there, you have to call their awareness to it. I prefer national campaigns, for reasons I've already discussed. However, local campaigns are still very valuable! Because the media looks at other media for stories and inspiration, local campaigns can become national overnight, and I've seen it happen.

But whether your story is mentioned in either a local or national medium, make sure everyone on social media knows about it. Talk it up in emails that go out to customers, potential customers, and other media targets that you want to interest. Contact other media outlets and introduce them to the story. This, and other methods, will be examined more closely as we go further into this book.

WHAT MEDIUM IS RIGHT FOR YOUR MESSAGE?

Not everyone is interested in the same message. Sometimes, even when classic publications or online news services aren't interested in a particular message, radio and podcasts or even TV and online shows may be! Some messages are a great fit for all of them. But do your research in advance, so that you can discover which ones will be receptive to what you have to say.

It's always a good idea to know your audience. So, let's talk a bit about who's out there and what they listen to and like to read.

Publication Demographics

Print media audiences (both online and offline) will vary depending on whether it's a newspaper, magazine, or a free publication. There are two main demographics to consider; the readership and the circulation. This can vary immensely from region to region, so you might want to find out who reads the particular newspaper that is available to your market before making any decisions about whether or not it's a good target for you.

According to Reuters, 20 percent of American readers paid to read newspapers online.

That sounds small, until you realize that it translates into over 66 million people that read these newspapers. That's a lot of people who could read what you have to say.

Circulation is a bit more difficult to determine. If the paper is also online, the online subscribers may or may not be the same as the people that get the paper delivered. In my company, when we consider newspaper demographics, we usually only count what their online readership is. Why? Because people that have the newspaper delivered almost always have an online subscription to that same paper and read their stories online, also.

Magazines and free publications don't necessarily have the same demographics as newspapers do. Like newspapers, however, they usually have an online presence, and with a little research you can discover more about their readers and the topics they specialize in.

I would caution you to not get too granular, however.

Remember what I said about charity? For example, you may view the *Wall Street Journal* as a business-focused newspaper and so you may feel that there would be no interest in your story about how volunteering at a charity makes people feel more fulfilled. But that would be shortsighted, because businesses know that charity is good business. Charities may not be intrinsic to how businesses operate, but businesses that are media savvy want to be seen as charitable. Additionally, good businesses want their employees to be happy and employees are increasingly demanding time off for charitable work.

In other words, be creative and don't automatically assume your story can't be shared. Look for the angles.

Demographics for TV and Online Shows

The demographics of TV and online show audiences really vary. There are shows out there for every and any topic and audience. When you are setting out to achieve publicity in these mediums, demographics will become extremely important. You'll want to determine who watches these shows and then use that information to select the outlets that will be best for your story.

At one time, the majority of daytime TV was targeted toward stay-at-home moms. But more recently that audience has shrunk to women over the age of 55 (*Wall Street Journal*). A secondary audience would be college students, who enjoy game shows in those time slots.

The news (both local and national) is watched by people of all ages. 16% of Americans primarily get their news from cable television news. That's over 53 million people and traditionally they've been age 55 and older. However, the landscape is changing.

"Fox News Channel dominated the cable news competition in the second quarter of 2021, winning across all metrics: among total viewers in prime time and daytime, and among viewers 25-54, the demographic group most valued by national advertisers." (*Forbes*)

As for the traditional TV news market, the Pew Research center reported that in 2020 ABC evening news viewership grew 16% to 7.6 million viewers. CBS evening news viewership grew 7% to about 5 million viewers, and NBC viewership rose 8% to 6.5 million people. Some of this was probably due to the fact that 2020 was an election year. Another contributing factor was the emergence of COVID-19. However, COVID-19, and all its variants, isn't going away. Politics is also more heated than ever, and it's likely that viewers will continue to tune in.

Demographics for Radio Shows and Podcasts

Let's say you have a story about how to best use social media in business. Since it's a topic that appeals to a lot of business-people, business radio would be a great choice. But if your story is about kids who are going away to college soon, you may want to consider pitching to a radio show that deals in family topics.

It used to be that radio audiences were skewed predominantly toward older male listeners. However, that's no longer true.

In "Weekly radio reach in the United States as of June 2021, by age and gender," Statista.com noted that "During an average week in June 2021, radio reached 88.1 percent of all American men aged between 35 and 64 years of age. All adults of this age group were the most exposed to radio, regardless of gender. The largest differences between the genders were between the oldest adults, with men aged 65 and over four percent more likely to listen to the radio."

But, what's even more exciting to see is the growth of the podcast.

"In 2021, the number of monthly US podcast listeners will increase by 10.1% year-over-year (YoY) to 117.8 million. Podcasts are mostly seeing traction among younger consumers—this year, more than 60% of US adults ages 18 to 34 will listen to podcasts monthly." *(Insider Intelligence)*

A podcast is a digital audio file created from a series of audio files that contain episodes. The podcast can be easily downloaded through the internet and can be listened to repeatedly or even listened to offline without an internet connection. This allows podcast audiences to listen at their convenience.

Podcasts are said to have been in existence since 2005, but they did not become popular until the podcast platform podcastone.com was founded in 2006. In a podcast, you can choose the order of your episodes or listen to them randomly.

Podcasting is not limited to the larger and more well-known podcasts. Anyone with a computer, internet access and recording software can create a podcast as long as they are able to create audio files.

The podcasting phenomenon has changed the way podcast listeners consume information through podcast subscriptions. With podcast subscriptions, podcast listeners subscribe to podcasts they want to listen to, and the podcast is downloaded automatically when a new episode appears on their subscription list. This allows them to have episodes ready to listen to at their convenience without having the need to actually search for it, and then wait for the podcast episode to download.

This means that there will likely be podcasts receptive to your message. It also means that if you find yourself enjoying the interview experience, you may even choose to start your own podcast.

HOW TO ANGLE AND PITCH
ONLINE AND OFFLINE PUBLICATIONS

We do it all the time, and you can do it, too, if you do it right.

You need to know your publications well enough to know which journalists specialize in your topic. The next step is to write a short, objective article about it. Have one or two people proofread it, and then email that story to your chosen journalists.

Make sure you have your bio at the bottom of the email, as well as contact information including your phone number. Sometimes a journalist will prefer to pick up the phone and call you before they take the time to email back. With any luck, and a bit of hard work, your articles will spark interest.

Do your best to tie your message into current events and/or news. If you can't do that, look for a topic that is universal.

For example, if you're an accountant, there isn't usually a great deal out there in the nightly news that would demand an accountant's hot take. But if you're comfortable talking about the ramifications of a particular tax dodge, or changing tax laws, there's always interest. People want to know how to keep their taxes low and they also want to know what to avoid. So, good news! You don't have to be interviewed only during tax time (in fact, I know you won't have time to do it during tax season).

WHY TALK INTERVIEWS CAN PROPEL YOUR MESSAGE

I asked our Talk Director, David Purdy, to weigh in on his personal experiences in radio. Dave is a US Navy veteran with a background in radio. His golden voice has been used in both radio and voiceover work. He is experienced both at the mic and in the production room. He is particularly knowledgeable about what sells in radio, and how to position the client's messaging to get them the maximum, effective publicity possible.

Over my career, I've been a DJ, traffic reporter, news anchor, show host, and producer. I've seen the value that guests bring to talk shows, which is why I went into the publicity field.

I introduce clients as authorities to be interviewed on radio and podcast shows, because I've seen how those interviews establish our clients as authorities worth listening to.

I'm going to tell you exactly why you should consider

advertising yourself as an expert, open to being interviewed on talk shows.

When I began my career, there were many talented people who worked in radio. As the years went by, technology advanced. Radio stations consolidated. My first radio job as an overnight DJ was replaced by a satellite show, which was shared with many other stations. It was an inexpensive alternative to every station paying for their own DJ talent. Instead of thirty DJs, suddenly thirty stations had just one.

In fact, stations (like all businesses) are notorious for finding the cheapest solutions possible. Even when I was a traffic reporter, I was on multiple stations under a variety of names, so it seemed like every station had their own reporter. During that time, I was on the oldies station, the classic rock station, a religious station and many others. However, the average listener had no idea this was happening.

Because stations always look for cost effective solutions, one interview may end up being played on many stations, or replayed when a station needs additional material. This means it's a golden opportunity for anyone that's been interviewed on these shows. Their message can spread quickly!

It's also wise to consider interviews on podcasts, which have grown in popularity over the recent years. This gives you even more opportunities to be heard. Often, both radio interviews and podcasts can be found on the internet (where you can link to them on your website) or you can record them and use snippets of these interviews to share on social media or in other marketing campaigns. This enables you to achieve an even broader audience than the original one you spoke to.

It's important to remember that both radio shows and podcasts must cultivate and keep an audience. We sometimes have clients that we want to schedule on a radio show, and the client says, "oh that's not my audience! They won't be at all interested in what I have to say!"

However, the truth is very different. These shows know exactly who their listeners are, and they won't put anything in front of the listener that they feel would hurt their show in any way. Measuring audience size is a science for people in radio. In radio, you live and die by ratings. So if they want you, you can be sure that their audience is also your audience.

And radio is still going strong these days. IHeart alone has over 850 radio stations.

Pew Research reported:

"The audience for terrestrial radio remains high, though there was a slight drop in 2020: In 2020, 83% of Americans ages 12 or older listened to terrestrial radio in a given week, a figure that dropped slightly from 89% in 2019 according to Nielsen Media Research.

As of 2021, 41% of Americans ages 12 or older have listened to a podcast in the past month, according to "The Infinite Dial" report by Edison Research and Triton Digital, up from 37% in 2020 and just 9% in 2008."

Radio is anchored to many people's daily lifestyle patterns. Tuning in to a preferred station is a reflex gesture for most of us, especially when it comes to hearing our favorite hosts live.

No matter how much time I spent on the radio, I still get exhilarated when I see the famous "Live Broadcast" sign! Even though our clients almost always interview over the phone, it still is one of the most exciting things you can experience.

Although they're similar, podcasts are very different from radio shows.

While radio can include pre-recorded content, many shows are usually live broadcasts, with an audience actively listening in at the time of your interview. Listenership of radio is still high, in fact, in 2020, 83% of Americans 12 or older tuned in at least once a week. By way of comparison, As of 2021, 41% of that same group have listened to a podcast in the past month.

Live radio can't be edited while it's being broadcast, but

podcasts are usually pre-recorded so that their listeners can download the podcast and listen at their leisure. This allows you to have a little more flexibility, if necessary, and makes it easier to correct mistakes or make adjustments afterwards.

And at this point, it appears that most podcast episodes will be online forever. That means your target audience will always be able to find your content.

Sometimes I'm asked about an audience size for a particular podcast. Usually, it's because a client is wondering if it's too small to be important. And that isn't always easy to determine.

You can get analytics from a number of different places, like the Google Podcast Manager, Apple and Spotify dashboards and, of course, your podcast host.

The problem is that podcast analytics are yet to be fully standardized across the board, meaning that downloads and listener numbers may not always be accurately measured. This causes a bit of a headache when trying to get an accurate picture of how a podcast is really performing.

I would never book anyone on a tiny show. However, I'll finish up with something that one of my colleagues recently said.

Before you turn your nose up at a podcast of 600 listeners, ask yourself this: Would you jump at an opportunity to speak at a conference where there were 600 people sitting there, waiting for you to get up and deliver your message? If the answer is yes, take the interview, no matter where it is in the country, and be glad that you didn't have to make the drive to get there.

This is the end of Dave's contribution. As you can see, his experience in both the radio and publicity industry is what makes his contribution so valuable. Dave has been able to strike up many friendships in the business, and talk show hosts know him by name and take his recommendations seriously.

HOW TO GET YOUR MESSAGE
ON THE RADIO AND ON PODCAST

Even if you don't have Dave's connections, here's how you can do something similar.

The writer that creates our articles is often the same one who works with me to design our radio and podcast pitches. When the pitch is ready, Dave then sends out the information to radio show hosts we know have been interested in similar clients or topics. He follows up with them regularly (it's important to establish strong relationships in this industry).

It usually works like a charm, bringing in interviews on major and syndicated shows across the country. On the rare instance that it doesn't work, we re-work the pitch and send it out again. It never fails to get interviews. The wonderful thing about radio and podcasts is that there's a show, topic, and perspective for every one of us.

It's most likely you already listen to talk radio and/or podcasts. Although I'm a voracious reader, I find that I can listen to similar content when I'm driving, cleaning house, or working out. You probably do the same thing. So, compile a list of everything you listen to throughout the day. Would those shows be interested in your message?

Put together an email to the shows you want to target. If you listen to them regularly and can truthfully say you're a fan, you can put that in your subject line or mention it at the beginning of your email. Be sure you can back that up, however. It would be pretty awkward to get a call from that show host only to have no idea what he's talking about. Give them 1-3 issues you can discuss on their show.

Remember that you are looking for publicity. This isn't marketing time. You shouldn't be selling anything. Instead, you are letting them know what issue you're an expert in, and that you have a solution to a problem.

Once you get on the show, it's important that you understand how to interview well. We'll discuss interviews later.

HOW TO GET YOUR MESSAGE ON TV AND ONLINE SHOWS

When you reach out to a show, chances are that you need to contact the show's producer. So it's always wise to research those shows, then conduct your campaign the same way you would conduct a radio campaign. And just like a radio pitch, be sure that your pitch is going to the right person about the right topic.

Local TV is a great way to start. You definitely want to have some local TV appearances before you try to take it to a national level. National producers want to see how you present yourself before they make any commitments.

Thanks to COVID-19, we can now be interviewed on TV without leaving the comfort of our home! And TV isn't the only place you can be seen. I've been interviewed by authors and companies that want an expert's opinion that they can share with their readers and clients. There are YouTube celebrities that also look for content for their platform. I even know one guy based in California that interviews different people on his weekly Facebook show. The topics aren't always the same. He just interviews who interests him.

Chances are, however, that you see appearing on TV as the pinnacle of success. And TV shows sometimes take advantage of that! There are some infamous shows out there that charge people to be guests. It's a lucrative model for them, but not always for the guest.

I was recently interviewed on a national TV news show. After the interview, I was emailed with their solicitation to spend between $500-$1500 to use that clip. I didn't purchase the clip because I have other ways to prove my authority. It might be the right choice for you, but it wasn't the right choice for me.

But there are still shows that don't charge you for interviews, and are looking for experts to come on and chat about solutions to the latest issues. And that's what you should focus on.

INTERVIEW TIPS

If you're an author, don't tell the listeners to buy your book. Give the host the chance to mention your name, credentials, and the book. If she forgets, then take the opportunity to work this information into your interview. But; don't cross the line and try to sell your book or anything else.

You see, if you want to sell a product, such as sweaters, you can speak about different types of yarn and what types are best for the consumer. You can speak about how sweaters are a great option in cold climates, and they beat dragging a blanket around all the time. What you *can't* do is tell everyone that Shantale's Sweater Shop is the best place to buy sweaters. That falls to marketing, and that's the kind of message you must pay for.

You must sell nothing except a realistic solution to a problem. That means that your particular brand of woven sweater can't be presented as the solution for everyone. If you make that mistake, the media will quickly file your story in the circular file and you won't hear from them again. However, people love to buy from people and organizations that they like, and when they look you up, they may just make the decision to buy what you're selling, even though you never asked them to.

No matter which medium you're interviewed in, you need to always remain professional. Don't get drawn into anything you shouldn't be speaking about.

I recently listened to a client being interviewed by a talk show host. The talk show host tried to tie his message into a particular political stance. The client dodged the question by not responding to the host's declaration. The host tried again, and that's when the client politely said he doesn't take political stands. It was an excellent way to handle the interview, and it kept the client from alienating people that needed to hear his message.

Most people realize you shouldn't swear during an interview. It's also wise to avoid slang, unless you're a pop star. And it's a good idea to practice with friends and family so that they can tell you if there's anything you might say that could cause confusion or annoy your audience.

I once had a client with a verbal tic. He kept saying "like" constantly (it was, like, almost every sentence). I was cringing by the end of the initial phone call. He wasn't a good fit for radio or TV, which are all auditory. However, I was able to get him in print stories where that verbal tic didn't make an appearance.

PRINT

With an interview that will land in a publication, there are times that a journalist will need to speak with you by phone or perhaps through a Zoom call. You can be pretty relaxed during this type of interview. It doesn't matter how much you clear your throat, if you have a verbal tic, or if you have to keep consulting your notes.

However, these interviews are usually conducted through email. If you're writing out your answers, proofread them before you send them back and then have someone else proof them also. If you're chatting by phone, make sure that what you say is clear and understandable. Have any facts, quotes or statistics on hand and be prepared to share them.

RADIO / PODCAST

Think of a radio interview as a chat between friends…with hundreds or thousands of people watching you. No pressure, right? But the reason I say this is to keep you focused on the audience. Make friends with the host, be engaging and interesting and keep your focus on her. But don't forget you're speaking to many others. Donald Trump made that mistake repeatedly with Howard Stern, and those mistakes continue to haunt him.

Unlike TV interviews, the audience can't see you turning pages to find statistics or taking notes. So, definitely have a notepad with a pen nearby so that you can jot down questions or thoughts that occur during the interview. This way you can stay focused on the host's questions and not get lost or forget a question.

Speak slowly and carefully. We all speed up when we're excited, and almost everyone speeds their speech up when they're on the radio. Practice, in advance, with your friends or family. Record your mock interviews and play them back so that you get used to how you sound. I've never met one person who thinks they sound better on radio or TV. In fact, I usually hear "Do I sound like *that*?" But, these practice sessions can help you discover if there's a word you use too much, or if you have a verbal tic that you have to work on.

The first time I was interviewed in a radio studio, I was mortified by the playback. I swore I'd never do it again. But I did. And eventually I had my own show. I still get interviewed on radio sometimes and I admit my voice is never what I would like it to be, but I've grown accustomed to it and it no longer makes me break out into a cold sweat when I hear it.

TV AND ONLINE SHOWS

TV and online appearances are often the *last* step to a successful campaign. The media wants to see you in print, hear your voice on the radio, and see your appearances in smaller forums before they ask you for an interview. Of course, there are rare exceptions, but you can't count on those.

When you feel you have enough traction to interest TV and/or online shows, it's time to pitch them the same way you pitch radio.

TV and online shows are similar to radio with one major exception: They're visual. That can be absolutely terrifying, unless you're a professional, but even pros get stage fright. Barbara Streisand is notorious for it. Even though I'd appeared on TV many times before, when I was recently interviewed for a national show, I found myself struggling *(live, on air)* to find a simple word! As I struggled, it got worse, until I forced myself to focus on a substitute word so that I could move forward.

Let me also tell you that the vast majority of people aren't supermodels or TV anchors. Don't compare yourself to the Kardashians. Instead, look around at your friends and colleagues. My guess is that there's a wide variety of looks, shapes and sizes. Viewers don't expect perfection. They want authenticity. They want to hear from authorities, and they know that authorities come in all packages. I have tons of clients tell me "I have a face for radio." But that's simply not true for them or for you.

So how do you appear your best? Wardrobe is important. Avoid stripes and plaids (sometimes they look wonky on camera). Also avoid trendy clothes unless you're being interviewed about this season's fashions. You don't want your clothing to be distracting. Instead, wear something that you would wear to the office if you're meeting with a client, and bring a change of clothes, just in case.

There are some colors to avoid. Yellow never looks good on anyone. Ever. Also avoid bright red or pink because they throw the camera off and your skin tone will take on a bizarre cast. Neons are also out for the same reason. It's OK to stand out, but you don't want to stand out like *that*.

Consider your message.

If it's somber, consider wearing clothes that are more subdued. Or do you want to appear approachable? Then perhaps dress less formally (think business casual). The best colors are the standard business wardrobe colors: Black, white, navy, cream, khaki, brown, pale pastels. Avoid splashy prints, even if the style is professional. I don't care what the news anchor on channel 9 was wearing yesterday. You aren't the anchor and, for all you know, her producer dragged her aside later to tell her that she should never wear that dress again.

Assume you're always being recorded. Always. How many times have we heard of someone who says something absolutely awful because they didn't realize they had a hot mic? Don't be that person.

Make sure you have your facts memorized and, if you can't do that, keep them on small note cards in case you have to reference them.

Stay focused on the host and listen carefully. Make sure you're answering the question that was asked, and nothing more. You'll never get asked back if you suddenly go off on a tangent.

Like me, if you suddenly find a brain freeze, attempt to give your answer a different way or ask the interviewer to rephrase it, in order to give you additional time.

Smile when you can, be personable and charming. Be yourself. If you try to be anyone else, you'll end up regretting it. But be your very best "you."

CHAPTER 6

MARKETING BASICS

Marketing is a way to persuade people to buy from you. Where publicity is more subtle, marketing usually isn't shy about telling consumers that they need to spend money on you or your product.

Sometimes marketing and publicity cross over. One example is social media, which can feature both publicity ("Dr. Metcalfe was just honored by *Physicians Monthly*") and advertising ("Mention you saw this ad to get 20% off!").

I'm going to discuss marketing from the viewpoint of someone who's conducted successful marketing and publicity campaigns. My goal is to show you how marketing campaigns can use your publicity effectively. That, combined with a good sales team, can create a powerhouse which will drive sales.

Marketing is paid-for advertising, and budgets can get out of control quickly. There are many ways to market simply and relatively cheaply. But remember the old saying "You get what you pay for." It usually takes money to make money. However, there are some methods that are more cost-effective than others.

Social media marketing is an example of one of the less expensive options. It can be effective because you can spend money wisely, getting your messaging to a target audience. You can also set a budget to prevent overspending, and conduct A/B testing, which will give you almost immediate results so that you can easily make adjustments. A billboard for example, is less of a known factor. You must take the billboard company's data at face value, and hope that your message will result in a return in sales that makes it a good investment.

WHY YOU NEED PUBLICITY
IN YOUR MARKETING STRATEGY

Publicity enhances marketing, but marketing can directly drive sales. The primary goal of publicity is to create an impression about you and/or your firm or product. Remember that publicity is about earning your way into media that can't be purchased.

The ultimate goal for every marketing campaign will always be sales. However, the underlying goals must be to establish credibility, prove worth, and get data for further marketing campaigns. Effective publicity can give you a much-needed shortcut, here. Take your hard-won publicity and incorporate it into your marketing materials to show that you've earned the right to be viewed as an authority. It gives the customer the reassurance that you're no fly-by-night.

I used to have a radio show that was sponsored by a particular company. Because that company was my sole sponsor, they made good use of it. They did video and audio recordings of the show, and then spliced the best parts into easy and topical soundbites. They put it up on YouTube (you can still find some there) and promoted them repeatedly across social media. They are an insurance company that could truthfully say "We're the insurance company behind The Business Edge radio show!" And that's just one example of how publicity can be used in your marketing efforts.

MEASURE YOUR SUCCESS
THROUGH YOUR RETURN ON INVESTMENT (ROI)

You can demand more quantifiable measurements from marketing than you can from publicity. So, no matter what you try, you can and should tie a revenue goal to marketing campaigns.

Although marketing usually means an outlay of cash to advertise, you absolutely can correlate ad performance to sales so that you can justify every dime you spend. This is known as the Return on Investment (ROI).

To calculate ROI, you take the sales growth from each business or product line, then subtract the marketing costs, and divide the total by the marketing cost for that business or product line. The formula is (Sales Growth - Marketing Cost) / Marketing Cost = ROI.

Why do you want to understand this calculation?

The general rule is that for every five dollars spent on marketing, the organization should expect to get back one dollar. And anything below a 2:1 ratio is usually seen as not profitable.

To figure out your ROI, you'll need to know which sales are a direct result of your marketing. That's why it's so important to track your promotions any way you can. If you're running ads on a social media platform, they usually can provide statistics that show you how well a campaign is going. If you're running a Google ad, they'll give you data also, including the click-thru rate. (Click-thru rate means how many people have clicked on your ad to go to your website).

MARKETING GURUS CREATE A UNIFIED STORY AND APPROACH

You can't just jump and build your wings on the way down. You'll live to regret it. A marketing campaign must start with the basics, first.

Successful marketing and publicity campaigns must be in step with each other. There needs to be an agreement about what you wish the world to see. This means you want to have a corporate style guide.

STYLE GUIDES

Why a Style Guide? A style guide is a formula for consistency. What rules make sense in your organization's marketing materials? Rethink what you've already done and be prepared to throw it away if it's not working, no matter how much you're in love with the concept.

Instead ask yourself what is mandatory in all marketing and publicity campaigns. Do you have a word or phrase that you want regularly emphasized or repeated? What are your web standards? Is your company voice playful? Serious? What are the primary colors or type fonts that must be used in all marketing literature? Is there anything that should be always avoided? What other basics should everyone agree upon?

How can you make sure that no one forgets the standards once they are established? Just as importantly, how will you give everyone the information they need, from copywriters to designers to sales reps?

Easy. They'll be in your style guide.

Style guides are standards for consistency in messaging of all types. Not enough companies have them. But even when a company's marketing and/or publicity departments have a style guide, it's treated as a well-kept secret. Of course, the entire style guide doesn't need to be shared with everyone in the company, but certain parts should be mandatory (such as communication styles, customer service policies, etc.)

Everyone with a publicity, marketing or sales position should be in unison about how to publicly represent the company. Remember, there's no "I" in "team," but there is a "me" in there. Individuals can often go off message if they're not reminded. So keep that style guide fresh in everyone's minds, reiterate your standards regularly, and if anyone goes off message, point them to the style guide.

QUESTIONS FOR YOUR STYLE GUIDE

Here are some of the questions that we ask our clients every time we bring them on board. These questions will help you as you decide what you need in your particular style guide.

1. What image and voice are you projecting? What's the look and feel of your brand?
2. Who is your target audience?
3. What benefits and advantages does your company offer to the consumer?
4. What are your customer service standards and procedures?
5. What emotions do you want people to feel when they hear your message?
6. What is your corporate personality? (ex. playful, energized, serious)
7. What action verbs do you usually use to describe your company or product?
8. What potential risks are you facing?
9. What SEO and social media practices are you following? What needs to be improved?
10. Do you have any copy or content guidelines?
11. What are the credentials of your spokesperson or owner?
12. Is there any negative press about your company? Where can it be found?
13. Is there anything your company won't discuss?
14. List prior media attempts at exposure. What worked? What didn't? Why?
15. What are the primary goals of the upcoming campaigns?

CORPORATE VOICE

Corporate voice is key to consistency and can be a winning part of every strategy. Wendy's is famous for their quirky voice on Twitter. Their interchanges and zingers make them a must-follow for many people. Not everyone can afford to have such a playful attitude, though. The general rule of thumb is the more expensive or serious the product, the more seriously it behaves.

If you're an author, you also need to decide what your voice is. One of my colleagues put it this way recently: Is your company humor sarcastic, lighthearted (i.e., "Dad humor"), or clever (wordplay, geeky references)?

Humor can be useful, as long as you're not covering a serious topic. But if you're a gastroenterologist discussing stomach cancer, there's no room for jokes.

Whatever voice you settle on, don't deviate from it.

TAKE YOUR LOGO SERIOUSLY

I often see small businesses with badly designed logos. It can be difficult to persuade a company to change the logo for a variety of similar excuses:

Excuse: It's already on our stationery and it will be too expensive to reorder all that stationery.

Answer: We don't use stationery as much as we used to. You can either reorder less stationery with the new logo, or use up current stationery until it's time to reorder, then order stationery with the new logo.

Excuse: The owner designed it (or Uncle John designed it, etc.).

Answer: This is business. There's no room for sentiment. It's time for a facelift.

Excuse: It will cost money to have someone redesign the logo.

Answer: Shop around for the right graphic artist but take it seriously. This logo represents you. You want to give the best first impression you can give. Yes, it will cost money. However, what is the cost of looking unprofessional?

Oh yes: There's always an excuse. But if you're motivated, you will find an answer. Don't let an outdated or amateurish logo give your customers the wrong impression about you. And make sure the redesigned logo is in a set of colors that you add to your style sheet so that you will have consistency in all your future marketing materials.

USE OF COLOR IN MARKETING

The more you use a consistent company color palette in everything you produce, the better. "Color improves brand recognition by up to 80%," according to *SmallBizGenius.net*.

Over the years, I've written many articles about the use of color in marketing, and they've been published in newspapers and online. But color psychology is always changing, and data continues to develop which shows that some of the initial findings were wrong.

For the longest time, yellow was a huge no-no. Everyone was told to avoid it or use it sparingly. Post-It Notes were an example of how yellow called your attention to something, but we also were told that more fights break out in yellow kitchens. Yellow was supposedly an irritant. It turns out that this misinformation, based on flawed studies, was wrong. I would still recommend limited use, however, and you'll soon learn why.

I've seen marketing materials that were significantly hampered by their misuse of color. You need to know your market. I was once asked to give my opinion on a book cover that was predominantly teal (a.k.a. turquoise). But what does teal indicate to the average viewer? We know women are very attracted to it, but men are equally repelled by it. The target audience was male, so I advised against the cover design.

We know that the universally preferred colors are blue, followed by green. Therefore, when she was going through this manuscript, my editor was somewhat confused. How could these two colors be so popular but, if mixed together, so polarizing?

VMG Studios may have the answer: "Color vision depends on color cones in our eyes, which are carried on the X-chromosome. Men only inherit one X-chromosome instead of two, as women do. These cones tell our brains what color we are experiencing by interpreting wavelengths of light.

Because men don't inherit the same combinations of cones women do, men's brains often require slightly longer wavelengths of light to experience the same colors. The article suggests this may be why men prefer colors with short wavelengths, like darker shades of blue and green, or they prefer shades without any wavelengths at all, like white, black, and gray."

Although blue and green top the list, almost everyone universally dislikes brown, orange, and the infamous yellow. Some evolutionary psychologists suggest that it's because these are the colors of decay. Our ancestors definitely needed to be able to recognize blue skies and green vegetation, which are representative of a healthy environment. They also needed to understand that rotting things signified unhealthy choices and surroundings.

Even if your heart was set on using brown, yellow, or orange, they can be used in moderation. For example, this book's cover is both the very popular sky blue paired with orange. The contrast is attention getting, and logical, since orange is the opposite of blue on the color wheel. They are two directly opposing colors, which are acceptable in color design. And there are still many colors you can choose from which may be highly effective in your marketing designs. Be careful, since some give certain impressions that could hurt or help you. Red may be a good color for a sale item, but it might be the wrong color for a boat company's logo. Take the time to do some research.

For current information on how to use colors wisely, I highly recommend the book *How Colors Affect You: What Science Reveals*, by William Lidwell.

GUERILLA MARKETING CAN BE A CHEAP OPTION

Of course we all look for inexpensive options, so let's get something out of the way. Guerilla marketing is an infamous, inexpensive marketing tactic, but it doesn't always pay off.

Guerilla marketing became popular in the early 90s. It's a combination of low to no-cost tactics and often it's unconventional. Because it's unconventional, it's also unpredictable. It may work, or it may not. It usually is creative and somewhat, well, downright sneaky at times.

For example, one product paid some of the prettiest sorority girls to pitch it on campus. It spread like wildfire, from campus to campus and sales shot through the roof. But another guerilla marketing campaign that did almost the same thing never took off. Usually, guerilla marketing works best in regional scenarios, like a local restaurant that needs more patrons. Rarely do you hear of a successful large-scale nationwide campaign.

I've personally had mixed success with guerilla marketing, but one successful campaign really stands out for me.

One year I was laid off. I had been the Marketing Director for a custom home builder that had hit hard times. As a struggling single mom, I needed a job and I needed it fast. The first job that was offered was an executive assistant position for a Vice President at a national car rental company. I took it and was glad to have it.

However, they soon realized that I was able to answer the phones, keep a calendar, and create marketing materials and ad copy. I was also consistently cheerful and worked hard. One day the V.P. called me into his office to tell me that he had just created a position and I would be the first person in that position. I became the first Convention Sales Director in the entire company, which is a position that continues today.

Well, that was just great! Except... what was a Convention Sales Director?

It turned out that they didn't have much of an idea about it, either. The basic goal was to convince local hotels and convention centers to part with their guest lists. I would then get in touch with the brides, the wedding planners, and the conferences that were flying in to enjoy our tropical weather and beaches.

No one was sure how to persuade them to do this, however. That was up to me. Oh, and I had almost no budget whatsoever. On the other hand, I got some pretty cool business cards out of the deal.

Well, I had to live up to those business cards. So I started making flyers and driving all around the beach side of the Tampa Bay Area (Pinellas County). I also faxed and emailed those flyers and soon every hotel and every convention center, every wedding planner and every music venue knew about me.

My little budget allowed me to buy candy bars at the local dollar store so I bought cases of chocolate candy bars, all types, and taped that business card to every one of them. Then I passed them out to all the "little people" that are so often ignored: The valets, the bellboys, the maids, the cooks and servers in the hotel restaurants. (Incidentally, this example shows why this book covers publicity, marketing and sales. It's a classic example of how effective they can be when they're combined).

Soon the sales came rolling in. In fact, it was so successful that there were days I had to scramble to coordinate all the different branches and get the necessary number of cars to a particular convention or wedding. It was the first time I'd experienced wild success due to some clever little flyers printed on the office copy machine combined with a bit of shoe leather.

As a result, other positions were opened in other regions and I trained the new Convention Sales Directors in these guerilla marketing tactics, which they used with success.

Other types of guerilla marketing include catchy videos that will hopefully be shared, publicity stunts, and other ways to inexpensively advertise on a large scale. A guerilla marketer might pay a local store to let them write a big message about their product on the store windows. Or, they might persuade a high school chorus to add their company jingle at the end of their holiday recital.

BUT WHEN GUERILLA MARKETING FAILS, IT FAILS SPECTACULARLY

I find guerilla marketing to be nerve wracking. It often fails more than it succeeds, and sometimes there can be terrible pushback. A stunt can backfire if it looks like a mean-spirited prank. And make no mistake: Even if you don't pay cash to advertise, you're paying someone to do all the work (even if that someone is you).

Here's an example from one of my failures.

Some time after working for the rental car company, I worked as a director at an employee leasing firm, which sold insurance as part of their package. The company wanted me to get an insurance license, and I got one. For many years afterwards, I maintained that license because I figured it was something to fall back on if I ever needed it.

One day it came in handy. I was approached by a family that owned a number of funeral homes. They wanted to create a job for me, specifically, and they wanted to target prepaid funerals for military veterans.

The goal was charitable. The government actually doesn't pay for military funerals, and many people are surprised when they hear this. The government may provide a plot to be buried in (or a spot for cremains), but they pay for almost nothing else. That means caskets, funeral home costs, cremation, urns, etc. are often unexpected expenses at the very worst time. Prepaying for your funeral arrangements means you can negotiate a better deal, and your heirs don't have to deal with funeral planning when they're already in mourning.

The idea was for me to recreate the same guerilla marketing campaign I'd done before, again with a very limited budget. However, the target was different. Instead of approaching businesses, we would target individual veterans.

I immediately ran into problems. Although the same shoe-leather/flyer scenario went into play, where would I take the flyers? We had wrongly assumed the VA would be happy to pass the information along, but as a government agency, they were not about to become part of a private company's marketing strategy. And though flyers could go up at the local VFWs, only a small percentage of veterans attended their events. It was difficult to know how to get the message out to veterans without a good advertising budget, which we didn't have.

Also, no one did any research on what the average veteran's finances looked like. In general, these elderly veterans struggled more than others in the same age group. Disabled veterans, the primary target, were interested but had no money whatsoever to prepay for funerals. They were lucky if they could pay next month's rent. Obviously, that meant that very few veterans could afford it. Therefore, even if every senior-age veteran in the Tampa Bay Area knew about prepaid funerals, most still would be unable to pay for them. I had some of these veterans tell me that they were going to donate their bodies to science to get around the problem. I had to be the one to tell them that they would be charged for even *that*. Instead of hope, I was sowing despair.

I sputtered along for three months, looking for any and all angles, until I gave up. It was a time of defeat and I felt demoralized. It was a waste of time and energy.

You could certainly argue that it wasn't the failure of guerilla marketing. Instead, we should have examined the market more carefully before we jumped in both feet first. But, there are many times when there simply isn't enough data or research available. Certainly at that time, there was no good data that we could find which would have shown us that our target audience was impoverished.

And although we weren't counting solely on the VA's help, it would have been a way to spread the message further than we were able to with our limited resources. Instead, we had assumed that the campaign would spread by word of mouth because we felt it was such a fantastic product! We were blinded by our own feelings about it, instead of looking objectively at the situation and digging around further to make sure we were right about what we believed.

Perhaps, most importantly, we were trying to reproduce a campaign that worked as a business-to-business campaign, but this was a business-to-consumer campaign.

This sad experience illustrates that the same type of guerilla marketing campaign doesn't work in all circumstances, and sometimes those circumstances aren't initially clear until it's too late. Also, I'm going to say this repeatedly: Times and methods change. Unless you have a crack team that is on top of it all, with a proven track record of success in guerilla marketing, it is a dangerous game to play. I personally don't recommend it.

PRODUCT CAMPAIGNS

Services can be difficult to sell, because you're selling an intangible. But, products are often easy to advertise, and even easier to sell. Obviously, ads can really drive those sales. However, an ad's call to action is usually something like "Click here to get 20% off! Offer expires in 24 hours!" Of course that means that you must be willing to discount your product to engage interest, but there's another way to drive interest without offering it at an initial discount. You can create something similar to a publicity campaign by getting your product on TV for free.

If you have a product that you'd like reviewed on a show, you can contact the show in advance and let them know what you have to offer. They may be interested in showing your product along with other products, and if they select your product, they'll be discussing it on air!

If your product is a summertime product (like a pool float) then get the information out to the stations way before summer hits. Shows like to plan way in advance, so make sure they have time to work your product into their lineup. For instance, shows begin to send out requests in August for products to review for their Christmas list recommendations. Very rarely will a last-minute item make it into these lists.

I once brought on a client that made specialty purses. The team faced a challenge, because her bags were a higher price point than those of her competition. However, they were a superior quality product: The vinyl was thicker, they were double stitched (not single stitched like their competition), and they were customized with unusual details such as a beautifully designed hangtag. We were sold on the product, but how were we going to sell others on it?

We started with a product pitch. We got the contract in late summer, just in time to get out the information to shows that talk about gifts to consider in the December holiday season. We also played up the details, which made this product truly exceptional. We ended up getting the purses reviewed on many shows.

However, we also conducted a publicity campaign. We went after other media by emphasizing the challenges of a small, family-owned business where other members in the family also worked side-by-side with the founder of the company. This two-pronged approach gave us a successful campaign.

USING YOUR EMAIL MARKETING LIST WISELY

Any time a client or potential client comes your way, make every effort to get their email address.

Customers appreciate it when you tell them that there's a sale (everyone loves to save money). But they also like it when you send them information that they can use, so share your blog posts with them. You can either copy and paste the blog post or write a short email and embed the link to the blog post.

And when you are featured in a news story or interviewed on a show, you can let them know about it by sending an email, too. This adds to your credibility and reinforces the idea that you are the expert in your field.

THE WONDER WALL

Not to be confused with the rock group, the Wonder Wall is that area that everyone sees when they first walk into your offices.

Now that so many of us work from home, you might choose to have it on the wall behind you so that when you're on a Zoom call everyone can see it. Let's face it: Those virtual background photos never look right in a Zoom call. When you're staring at someone during the meeting, and their edges blur into the background, it's distracting. But a Wonder Wall behind you is unique, and won't glitch out at an inconvenient moment.

Wherever you choose to locate it, your Wonder Wall is another piece of your marketing strategy. It should have all awards and all press clippings proudly displayed for everyone to see. If your Wonder Wall is looking pretty sparse, not to worry! Your publicity campaigns should be upping the supply regularly.

GIVEAWAYS: GIVE THEM A PASS

Although I primarily want to discuss how publicity should be positioned, I can't resist this word of caution about a certain type of marketing.

I write this with the hope that the newest strains of COVID-19 will eventually become obsolete and life will return to some semblance of normalcy. If we lose out on future conferences, they will be replaced by online events and giveaways will become something for the history books.

Any time you attend a conference where businesses are giving away pens, bags, and stress balls, you'll always hear someone say, "If it's free, it's for me." But is all this stuff (a.k.a. marketing collateral) really worth it?

There's a lot of data supporting it, but the data is suspect since it's mostly provided by companies that sell ...*(wait for it)*... marketing collateral.

The most recent and impartial article I could find from a trusted source came out in early 2021. Nowhere in that article was anything mentioned about giveaways. It was all about *online* marketing collateral.

At one time, studies repeatedly showed that people were more willing to buy from someone who'd given them something because they felt obligated to do so. This research was behind the long-standing belief that *anything* given away would create that sense of obligation. However, the modern consumer doesn't usually think like this.

For example, Groupon gained the reputation of being a place where companies could go to be quickly destroyed. You see, some companies made the massive mistake of offering freebies (through a binding contract with Groupon) to an unlimited number of people. These companies were severely impacted by this, and some went out of business as a result. You can't give out tons of freebies if they don't bring you business, obviously.

Groupon probably won't be around much longer. But the reason Groupon fell from grace was because of the damage that small businesses incurred when they cut those deals with Groupon. Those companies didn't realize that although people are always happy to get a freebie, many people can take advantage of it and it doesn't always translate to sales.

Every time I go to a conference or expo with giveaways, I see people grabbing what they can. But what happens next? They stuff everything into their suitcases, throw out anything that doesn't fit, and drag them home. Then these whatnots get passed off to kids or perhaps a colleague who will, in turn, pass it on to someone else or throw it in their desk. Eventually it gets thrown out when the annual office decluttering happens.

People don't want a mousepad on their desk with some random company's logo. If they're going to look at it every day, they want something that they can identify with like Mickey Mouse or a photo of their new puppy.

A stress relief ball (or any other creative shape) goes to the kids. Very few people actually pick one up at the office because they've had a stressful day and then, ahhhh, the stress goes magically away. It's really only a useless soft sculpture. Now if your target is kids, and it's a fun shape with bright colors, it might work, but it's still a long shot.

Pens are a bit more useful and if they're of good, long-lasting quality they'll be around longer. But I have pens that are labeled by many different companies and I've never thought "Oh, Mike's Air Conditioning. I should call them!" If I have an air conditioner emergency (obviously they happen here in Florida) then I call Dwight, who's been taking care of my AC units for years. If my friends have an AC emergency, they go on Facebook asking for recommendations and they're instantly flooded with them. No one says, "Oh hey, I have Mike's Air Conditioning on one of my pens. Why don't you try them?"

What is true for pens is true for other office supplies like branded Post-It notes, branded notepads, and more.

I believe marketing collateral is a huge waste of money. If you want to hand something out, hand out candy bars and business cards or brochures. Any time a vendor has candy, that booth is decimated quickly. Everyone likes candy. While they help themselves to candy, take the opportunity to pitch them your product.

I can think of one possible exception to this. I recently went to the state fair with my friend, Matt, and I came home with a very tiny colorful robot figurine that had been created by a 3D laser printer. My brother has been wanting one of those printers, and I passed the little thing on to him along with the group's information (it's a group of 3D hobbyists). To be fair, he hasn't joined the group or followed up with them. However, it was not just any giveaway. It was a small sample of the products they could create, so it was directly representative of them in ways that a mousepad or a pen are not. We'll talk about samples next.

But in all the history of giveaways, I've never had one person tell me or one of my salespeople, "Oh, I called because you're on my mousepad."

FREE TRIALS AND SAMPLES

However, free trials do have their use. They create an opportunity for a potential client to use your product for a brief amount of time. It needs to be a period of time that's long enough to let them see what the product can do, and short enough that they'll want more of it and be willing to pay for it. Free trials are great for software, which can simply lock out the user after the time has passed.

Free trials aren't limited to software. In fact, some companies have made huge profits from free trials. Ipsy and Birchbox are two companies that are middlemen (companies that stand between the manufacturer and the targeted user). They realized that people would pay for samples of bath products and cosmetics. They make arrangements with various manufacturers to get trial-sized items, and then bundle up whatever they're given into a monthly box that the client pays for. Obviously, the manufacturers are finding that it creates new clients. And these subscription companies find it to be very lucrative.

Of course, not everyone can offer a free trial. It would make no sense for a carpenter to offer a free trial, for example. But it pays to think outside the box. I'll bet you never considered that your car mechanic offered something like this. But car mechanics often offer cheap oil changes which are at cost so that you will come back to them when something serious happens to your car.

Aestheticians might offer a mini-facial at a low cost. Massage therapists might offer a ten-minute massage for free, or the first thirty-minute massage at a rock bottom price to entice the client to pay for additional time (and ensure future visits).

If you create beautiful pottery, you might want to pass out pretty pottery magnets or coasters with your logo on the bottom. If you're a glass blower, sell tiny glass animals at cost in addition to the big, beautiful vases.

But think it through carefully, and consider trying it out on a small audience before you do it on a larger scale. Your goal needs to be to create something that is representative of what you can truly produce, and not just a throwaway item.

THE OTHER TYPE OF MARKETING COLLATERAL

At all times, think about how you can incorporate publicity into your marketing collateral.

Marketing collateral has changed. It can be printed materials, like flyers and business cards. But it can also be online or offline media used to support the sale of a product or service. Marketing collateral includes an online video, a blog post, and yes, even an MP3 on Spotify. Marketing collateral accompanies every step in the sales process from beginning to end.

White papers are particularly valuable. "A white paper is a report or guide that informs readers concisely about a complex issue and presents the issuing body's philosophy on the matter. It is meant to help readers understand an issue, solve a problem, or make a decision." (Wikipedia)

Although it's tempting to avoid doing a lot of work on a give-away item, take the time to make the white paper representative of you and what you have to offer. Content quality is of utmost importance. When you're ready to share it with the world, offer it as valuable content on your website and/or through advertising. Someone who wants to read it will need to provide their email address, where you can send either the white paper or a password to view it on your site. This email address is an important asset. These people have shown that they're interested in your message, and will likely be receptive to regular updates, newsletters, and promotions.

Also consider both paper and online brochures, monthly newsletters (if they provide genuine value), case studies, infographics, and online sales presentations.

Whatever you choose, it's extremely important that your materials are kept up-to-date and relevant. They need to be re-examined regularly. Don't read this and say to yourself, "Yeah, yeah. Good idea." Instead, I would encourage you to immediately set up a review if you haven't done so recently. Also, you need to determine how often you should re-examine them and pencil it into your calendar now. Otherwise, one day you'll remember this and realize it's been five years since you read this book, and it is been neglected.

It's also imperative that you have consistency throughout all your materials, both online and offline. That means the same logo, same proportions, same text, and same color scheme (refer to the style guide mentioned at the beginning of this chapter.)

PULLING IT ALTOGETHER: PLANNING A SUCCESSFUL, HOLISTIC CAMPAIGN

After you've decided on everything you want to do, you need to create a marketing calendar. Don't be alarmed, it's nothing special. It's a regular calendar reserved only for marketing efforts.

It should include when blog posts go up, when social media accounts post content, when and where infomercials are displayed, when and where ads will run, and any other marketing efforts you're planning.

You can't really do this as easily for publicity, because publicity is more fluid. You never can be sure when an article will run in a publication, or when that next interview will happen. You will be able to use all of that publicity in your marketing campaigns, however! Keep a running list of all publicity exposure, and use it in your marketing attempts whenever possible. When you do, make a note so that you know what you used and where you used it. If you are posting regularly on social media, keep track of what you've mentioned and when you should post about it again.

CHAPTER 7

SOCIAL MEDIA
(FIRST IMPRESSIONS
ARE EVERYTHING)

Social media can be a great way to publicize your business for free. It's a combination of publicity tactics and marketing.

When you start to go after publicity, the media will begin investigating you by looking at your website(s) and social media pages/feeds. What they see will make all the difference about what types of opportunities you'll get. And remember that most customers will see them before they get in touch with you. Like your logo, those first impressions are invaluable.

But it's not always free. Social media platforms like Facebook, Twitter, LinkedIn, Instagram, and TikTok will all charge you to boost a post or display advertising. Still, there are some advantages. You can carefully choose your audience and keep your expenses limited to the groups you choose, and that's a big benefit.

WHAT IS SOCIAL MEDIA?

Social media is a catch-all phrase for any online platform that allows people to gather and socialize. There are many different platforms, and recently more have been popping up. TikTok has proved that there can always be a successful new player.

Over the last couple of years, there's been an increasing clamor against social media censorship. People have used these platforms for free for so many years that they've come to believe they're entitled to unrestricted access and the right to post anything they choose. The pushback against these platforms has been loud. However, it can't be denied that at this time all major platforms are privately owned, and they can place whatever restrictions they choose on their users until, and if, the government changes that through regulation.

Personally, I would prefer the platforms concentrate on monetization and avoid censoring anything but the most extreme content, such as violence or pornography. My view is that these platforms are similar to the phone company. People that pay to use a phone service are treated equally, and allowed full use of the service. There's no phone company that listens in on every conversation and hits a buzzer each time they hear something they don't like, right? Likewise, some pundits claim that these platforms are the digital equivalent of the town square, and traditionally town squares were places of uninhibited dialogue.

I would like to see these platforms set up a two-tier system. For a set fee, users can say what they want unless it's to promote or display extreme content. The users that choose to continue using the service for free will be at the mercy of the censors.

Although I think my idea is just fabulous, it doesn't look like any of the social media companies agree.

In the meantime, censorship has led some people to leave the most well-known platforms and begin to participate on lesser-known alternatives. However, *Fortune* magazine labeled this migration a temporary fad in May 2021.

Unless a user is severely irritated, it's highly unlikely they'll migrate. At best, some users currently seem to continue using the major platforms while dabbling in the others. For this reason, I'm only going to be concentrating on the major players. And, whether you like them or not, that's where business still is done.

Oberlo (whose parent company is Shopify) reports, "The latest figures show that there are 3.78 billion social media users worldwide in 2021—a five percent increase from a year ago. It is also 920 million more than the number of social users in 2017, which represents a whopping 32.2 percent jump in just five years.

The average annual growth rate over this period is 7.2 percent."

And yes, Facebook is still the market leader, with 68% of all US adults participating on the platform (Pewinternet). Any migration since that report would be miniscule, percentage-wise. From my own experience, I've seen people leave in a huff, swearing they'll never be seen there again. They usually announce a different social media platform where they'll be hanging out. And then they eventually creep back in quietly and everyone pretends they never left.

73% of marketers believe that social media marketing has been somewhat or very effective for their business. (Buffer) That makes sense, since each social media user spends an average of 2.5 hours on one or more social media platforms. (DataReportal)

91% of social media users get their fix through their cell phones. (*Lyfe Marketing*) Who's surprised? We see people on their phones everywhere we go. We've all seen videos of people who are so glued to their phones that they walk right into walls or ponds. So obviously, wherever they go, consumers can still see your messages.

Let's face it: Social media really has become a better version of the town square. You can see what your friend, Freda, is up to in Florida and at the same time you can also check up on Tom, who lives in New Hampshire. Your news feed will show Aunt Emma's photo of her new pottery painting business, and just below that you'll see an ad for the boutique deodorant soap you were considering. Should you get it this time, you wonder?

THE BIG 6

FACEBOOK

If you saw it on Facebook, chances were that you would end up getting that deodorant soap. Facebook has had some fantastic algorithms that effectively target the consumer. Once they knew what you were interested in, they made sure that you would have many opportunities to buy it.

All the major platforms are continually attempting to improve their algorithms. The giants have had a head start of epic proportions, and Facebook has been the titan among them all with a whopping 2.89 billion monthly active users.

The original Facebook was started in 2004 by several Harvard students. The most famous one is Mark Zuckerberg, who's currently the fifth richest person in the world. He didn't get rich by accident. No matter what you might think about him, he became rich primarily because Facebook users purchased products through ads on his platform. It's that simple. That alone should convince you that advertising and boosting posts on Facebook were, until recently, worthwhile.

However, as this book goes to print, controversy has cropped up. As late as 2019, Zuckerberg said at Georgetown University:

People no longer have to rely on traditional gatekeepers in politics or media to make their voices heard, and that has important consequences. I understand the concerns about how tech platforms have centralized power, but I actually believe the much bigger story is how much these platforms have decentralized power by putting it directly into people's hands...We can continue to stand for free expression, understanding its messiness, but believing that the long journey towards greater progress re-

quires confronting ideas that challenge us. Or we can decide the
cost is simply too great. I'm here today because I believe we must
continue to stand for free expression.

Yet by Fall of 2021, Facebook finally revealed that they now are favoring the major news media players, are prioritizing (somewhat restricted) interactions between individual users, and have claimed that their overarching goal is to "foster a safer community." It also has been revealed that Facebook has a censorship tier system. Citizens of some countries, such as America, are carefully scrutinized and monitored, while citizens of other countries, such as Ethiopia, have almost no restrictions.

These changes are concerning. Yes, everyone agrees that a safe community dialogue is a wonderful goal, but what exactly does that mean? So far, Facebook doesn't give any guidelines.

52% of all Facebook users get their news through their Facebook newsfeed. Over the years, I've grown to know many small publications that are struggling to remain relevant. Many of them have a shoestring budget and their niche audiences are usually local or unique in some way. These publications barely survived the industry-wide acquisitions, mergers, and layoffs, but this could be the final blow. Due to these new regulations which negatively target independent news sources, they have little chance of getting noticed. Their stories will never make it into people's news feeds, even if they're well-sourced and factual.

However, even if their stories *do* make it into the feeds of their target audience, they have yet another problem.

Facebook users will now be mostly hidden from their friends' newsfeeds if they share a lot of stories and links. Therefore, those of us who used our daily feed to share interesting articles will now be rarely seen. I used to share articles on marketing, publicity, and other interests. Since most of them have become invisible, why post at all?

Users that don't feel heard will gradually burn out and become inactive, unless Facebook rethinks this. I've already realized that I'm using Facebook far less than I used to. A social platform that is antisocial has no chance of growth. For example, Ebay was once the King of online e-commerce. However, they grew too comfortable, got greedy, and began to impose draconian regulations on their sellers. Now they are one of many options, and becoming increasingly irrelevant. When you lose sight of your true customer, you will never fully recover.

Facebook also admits that it now restricts "links to websites that receive a particularly disproportionate amount of their traffic directly from Facebook compared to the amount of traffic the websites receive from the rest of the Internet." This certainly will cause businesses to wonder if they should continue to advertise and interact on Facebook. It will benefit large corporations, such as Subway, who are already well established, while a small hometown deli will have no chance to be seen.

Additionally, due to this new prioritization of (somewhat restricted) individual interactions, corporate Facebook pages will be downrated, while Facebook private groups are becoming increasingly important.

At this point, it seems that individuals will only be able to speak somewhat freely in these private groups. This will likely drive people to interact only in their own selected groups, and public posts will decline. In a way, it could solve the censorship problem. Facebook censors have never been able to stay on top of all the material that was continually being posted. Now it will be up to group moderators to censor, instead. I suspect that this change will drive business representatives to join multiple groups, in order to network. Whether that will be a workable solution remains to be seen.

Many experts are alarmed: Will Facebook downgrade your entire company if you say anything that disagrees with their outlook? Is it still wise to spend your advertising budget there?

I believe these issues would be partially solved if Facebook chose to offer the individual user an opt-out of these new policies. However, this doesn't seem likely.

So-called whistleblower Frances Haugan claims that Facebook was responsible for the Capital riots of Jan. 6, 2021. Her motives are murky. In testimony before Congress on October 6, 2021, Haugan recommended that the government provide an oversight body for Facebook, suggesting that she, or someone like her, be put in charge. The problem is that Haugan was a simple product manager at Facebook, and not of expert status, so she's suggesting she get a promotion way above her abilities. This self-aggrandizement causes her recommendations to be suspect.

But, the government is becoming interested again. Will this lead to deregulation? More regulation? Only time will tell. So far, Congress regularly calls Mark Zuckerberg in, harrumphs noisily at him, threatens to regulate Facebook in some way, and then everyone forgets about it. However, if it leads to even further strangling of free speech, Facebook will soon not be a viable alternative for most people. It will merely be a place to post pictures and videos, and yet Instagram and TikTok both do it better. In the future, we may look back at this point as the death knell for Facebook. As of January 2022, Facebook is facing an antitrust lawsuit from the FTC, as the government has grown increasingly alarmed by it's seemingly endless expansion.

For now, there still is a great deal that attracts users to Facebook.

Yes, Facebook allows you to post photos and videos, but it also allows dialoguing and even long stories. One of the writers I work with is a poet that posts his content there regularly. As I mentioned earlier, they offer live, streaming feeds which can be used for everything from jewelry auctions to a type of visual podcast. I've "attended" a wild plant identification walkabout through the Florida wilderness with a pair of botanists one

Saturday morning. I wasn't the only one. It was a popular event.

"As of July 2021, it was found that 9.4 percent of total active Facebook users worldwide were women between the ages of 18 and 24 years, while male users between the ages of 25 and 34 years constituted the biggest demographic group on the social media platform," says *Statista.*

That's significant, because it was commonly believed that Facebook was losing traction with the Millennials and Gen Z. It's long been a favorite of Gen Xers, who were really the first on the platform. But Boomers also participate on Facebook. According to Pew, Facebook has the highest number of users in the 65+ and 50-64 age ranges.

In other words, if you want to target Millennial men or people age 50+, Facebook still may be an excellent choice.

LINKEDIN

LinkedIn had a rocky start in 2003. When it began, it was just a place to park your business profile. If you were looking for work, you could try to find business owners and employees that might listen to your pleas for a job. Initially LinkedIn looked like it was going to fail. However, it ultimately took off and performed so well that Microsoft bought it in 2016. It now has over 740 million users.

LinkedIn monetizes a bit differently than Facebook. In the last seven years, the majority of its profits come from selling information to recruiters and charging users for premium access and services (I personally pay for this, and I feel it's worth it).

Sometime in 2011 or 2012 (shortly after they began to exchange on the stock market) my friend, Tom Brown, told me that this was going to be huge. If you want to be taken seriously, he said, you need to hunt down colleagues and friends just like you do on Facebook. The more connections, the better, he added. That's when I began to look at LinkedIn again, and it's been a thriving social media platform ever since.

Now I have over 2,500 connections on LinkedIn. I treat it differently than I treated Facebook. Facebook was for friends and family. LinkedIn is your corporate image.

In some ways, I have LinkedIn to thank for my success. It's where clients go to leave reviews. It's where ideas and opportunities are shared. And it's also a great place to advertise!

Remember that 2020 was a huge blow to many companies, but LinkedIn reported $181 billion in revenue that year. LinkedIn continued to expand and reported a 23% increase in the first quarter of 2021. *Business Insider* has named it the most trusted social media platform.

The average LinkedIn user is wealthy, male, and well-educated (Pew Research). It's no surprise that LinkedIn is the most popular platform for B2B sales (Content Marketing Institute). If you're targeting businesses, this is the place to advertise. It certainly is the place to post, because you can post your articles for free and then share them everywhere. They can be shared on LinkedIn and other social media platforms, emailed to clients, and passed along by friends.

INSTAGRAM

This one was a real nuisance for the longest time because you could only easily interact with it on your phone, and I had the habit of checking my social media on my laptop during the day. Therefore, I just never really got into using it a lot and that habit (or lack of habit) stuck.

However, Facebook eventually purchased it. This brought up accusations of monopolization, but Facebook swore that Instagram would continue to operate independently. That didn't stick, but they're still very distinct platforms.

In March of 2021 Instagram launched a service that allows up to four users to interact via video feed. That is interesting but

I'm guessing the primary users will be pre-teens and teens. Businesses will continue to use Zoom or Google Meet, as those were the first major platforms for video calls.

There are 1.34 billion monthly active users. "25-34-year-olds represent the largest advertising audience on Instagram, followed closely by the 18-24-year old age group. Men slightly outnumber women in these age groups. However, women outnumber men among users 35 and up," according to Hootsuite.

The majority of Instagram users are young, educated females. Also, Instagram is most popular with Hispanic adults, followed by African Americans and Whites (Pew Research).

If your business, book, or message can be turned into a visual or a video, and your target audience meets these demographics, Instagram is one of the best places to post. Of course, you should also consider advertising on the platform.

If you're an event planner or a musician that needs to let his audience know where he's going to be next, you need Instagram. Over 75% of all people on that platform follow events such as conferences, concerts, and sports.

TWITTER

Twitter was introduced in 2006, two years after Facebook. Twitter's founders call Twitter a "micro blog." It's a way to get a message out in a powerful punch. While Facebook allowed more flexibility in posts, Twitter initially limited posts to 140 characters. It became a bit of a game to see how much of a message you could cram into that small space. Eventually the restriction was doubled to 280 characters. Most important messages can be kept to this length. The links that you attach and the hashtags that you embed also do some of the talking for you.

Although Twitter has had a steady growth in popularity since it was first created, of course it's the most notorious for being Donald Trump's social media platform of choice for many years. But in 2017, Sam Sanders of NPR reported that Trump really had no impact on Twitter's overall users, in part because people didn't have to belong to Twitter to hear of his latest tweets. News media all over the globe often reported the tweets in real time, so who needed an account?

Interestingly, Sanders added, "Debra Williamson, an analyst with eMarketer, says this kind of problem is not new for Twitter. "For as long as Twitter's been in existence, it's had far more popular awareness than it's had actual users," she says. "Everybody knows what Twitter is. But not that many people use Twitter. And they've been fighting that perception, which has turned mostly into a reality over the past few years.""

Yet Twitter still has an important part in any social media plan, due to 206 million very public users. In fact, because you don't need a Twitter account to view Twitter posts, the audience will likely be even larger.

Wordstream observed "It's true – Twitter has its problems, but in certain cases and contexts, it truly is the best ad platform you'll find – though ultimately it will depend on what you hope to accomplish. But Twitter offers some unique ad targeting features you won't find anywhere else."

And, unlike other platforms, you only pay for performance. This means that you only fork over the money when you got the results. Additionally, it's very easy to target (and micro target) your audience, and the rates are usually cheaper than many alternatives.

Here are a few things to be cautious about: Some words may not shorten well, such as associate ("ass"). Also, there are times that shortening a word will lead to a great deal of confusion, so stay alert. Donald Trump showed us that you can put out a chain of these tweets if you need to expand your message, but I don't recommend this. He also showed us that it's important to proceed with a certain amount of caution. If you aren't known for tact or witty repartee, let someone else run the company Twitter account. They can sweat the small stuff, while you kick back with a nice, hot cup of covfefe.

YOUTUBE

One of Googles' many captured companies is YouTube, which was started in 2005. It is the second most visited website worldwide, with over two billion monthly users. Most companies use YouTube, at the very least, as a place to house their video content. Then they embed those videos in their website or post them in their other social media accounts.

"54% of consumers would like to see more video content from brands they support," reports HubSpot.

And, "YouTube is most popular with users 35 and under, but only slightly. 73% of Americans aged 36 to 45 use YouTube, along with 70% of those aged 46 to 55 and 67% of those 56 and older. This is a very different pattern from other social platforms, where use drops off sharply in the older age group," says Hootsuite.

So, I encourage you to be adventurous and explore this option. You could begin by taping your own videos (or have someone record you) talking about your passions. Before you begin this, ask yourself what *you* like to see. Then ask the people you respect. These videos can be very short (think TikTok). However, many times a longer video can be successful on YouTube, if it's informative. But don't run on *too* long!

According to Visme.co, "The ideal length for a YouTube video is ten minutes. Generally, videos between seven to 15 minutes perform well on the platform. However, keep in mind that your video only needs to be as long as it needs to be."

Videos of up to fifteen minutes in length can be uploaded to YouTube. Verified accounts can post longer videos (up to twelve hours long). Like Facebook and TikTok, there's a live streaming option available in the USA and in many other countries. Although you have these options, use them wisely: Reward their trust in you by giving them quality content, in a concise or entertaining manner.

Take note of all the different types of videos that are shown on the platform and ask yourself how you might be able to tap into the variety. For instance, there are a lot of alternative music "channels" that broadcast through YouTube. YouTube is famous for the collaborative efforts that happen there. So if you have a music business that would sync well with, say, a talented artist that creates customized guitars, then it could be a great time to find this person and start your own channel with them.

I continue to be impressed by the Dr. Squatch ads (Dr. Squatch soap). They aren't done with a big budget, but the marketing team was savvy enough to hire a comedian to help create the commercials (he's also the spokesperson). Many people go out of their way to hunt down those commercials and watch them. I can almost guarantee you that there's a large number of people who continue to listen even after the timer's run out.

Even if you aren't placing any significant amount of content on YouTube, you still should consider creating a short video commercial that gets the most important information out in the first five seconds (before the viewer can click "skip" on a video). Make it enticing, so someone would want to continue to watch it before they move on to what they originally intended to view.

TIKTOK

TikTok is the new kid on the block but it's thriving among all age groups and sexes.

Variety recently reported, "The Chinese government has taken a stake and one of three board seats in a key subsidiary of TikTok owner ByteDance…" Yes, TikTok is owned by a Chinese company, and Chinese companies have always been carefully scrutinized and overseen by the Chinese government. And the Chinese government has a well-documented habit of human rights abuses.

This has resulted in a great deal of controversy ever since TikTok was released to the world in 2017. It's a known fact that TikTok is scraping users' data with a sophisticated set of algorithms that could make Facebook envious. And because TikTok doesn't have to conform to American rules, and isn't owned by an American company, there's little anyone can do about it. It would be up to the American government to step in, and at this time the current government doesn't seem to feel it's a threat. This could change, however.

Variety added further into their article that even though this latest news doesn't seem to immediately affect TikTok, "...the move comes amidst Beijing's broader campaign to exert greater control over its tech giants, curbing their influence with antitrust probes and increased regulations." What will this mean for the future privacy of TikTok users? We simply don't know. So, use at your own risk.

All that being said, I still have a TikTok account. It's important to remain on top of the trends, and this one is growing at an insane rate. Morning Consult ranked TikTok as the third fastest growing internet brand of 2020.

Additionally, TikTok is entertaining and, frankly, addictive. And it was designed to be. To be clear, all social media apps are designed to be addictive. However, TikTok has really mastered the concept. John Hermann of the *New York Times* noted in 2019, "Under the hood, TikTok is a fundamentally different app than American users have used before." Other social media platforms are taking note.

In that same article, Hermann quoted a social media specialist. ""It's doing the thing that Twitter tried to solve, that everyone tried to solve," he said. "How do you get people to engage?" Apparently you just ... show them things, and let a powerful artificial intelligence take notes. You start sending daily notifications immediately. You tell them what to do. You fake it till you make it, algorithmically speaking."

And that powerful AI is exactly why advertisers are also taking notice. This will allow you to pinpoint your target audience better than ever before.

The wonderful thing is that in the last year videos have been growing wildly in popularity, in part thanks to TikTok. We're seeing that all successful campaigns include lots of video content that can be shared on social media.

Incidentally, I recently had a client tell me that he didn't want to publicize on TikTok because his friends told him it wasn't a good fit for him. They told him he was too old, and that his message wouldn't appeal to Millennials or Gen Z. I had to disagree. TikTok increasingly has participation from all age groups, including Boomers. In fact, I follow one incredible dancer who's in his late sixties. But you don't have to dance to engage people on TikTok. So what happened? He found he had a whole new market on TikTok!

Show your fun side! People do all kinds of things on TikTok, from art and dance to practical jokes or demonstrating an unusual trait. If you're not comfortable doing any of that, give a quick minute chat about your topic, and do it with flair!

HASHTAGS AND TRENDS

You probably know what a hashtag is. But in case you don't, here's a quick summary. The # symbol is known as a hash sign. People that search for a particular topic on social media need to have an easy way to find it. The way to alert people that your post falls into the category they're looking for is to tag it. Therefore, a hashtag is a way to tag your post with a word that summarizes what you're trying to say, and you put the hash mark in front of the tag so that the search engines can easily find it.

A hashtag about publicity could be one or all of these: #PR #publicity #publicrelations. Hashtags about a new dinosaur fossil being discovered could be #dino #dinosaur #fossil #paleontology and those are just the most obvious.

Although you can post up to 30 hashtags at one time, it's not recommended. The recommended number of hashtags per post is between 1-3. Add too many and it looks desperate and obnoxious.

Some hashtags that are trending on one social platform may not be trending on another one. Make sure to adjust your hashtags accordingly, even if you're posting the same thing on each social media account. You can always google to see what hashtags are trending at the moment. However, most platforms are very helpful, and as you type your hashtag, they'll show you how popular it is, and often you can also see how many other posts include that hashtag.

Stay on top of trends and keep alert. You may find a trend that you can use. For example, I'm sure that AFLAC is anxiously waiting for #DuckLips to become popular again.

SOCIAL MEDIA BEST PRACTICES

Stay Away from Politics and Religion

In your personal accounts, do as you like. But in your commercial accounts, don't be political or religious unless your entire brand is political or religious. Why alienate large groups of people needlessly?

Develop Connections and Build a Following

From each account, follow other groups or individuals that might be interested in your product or messaging. Comment on what they have to say and share any of their posts that are relevant. Do be careful to do this only with sources that are respectable. The last thing you want to do is find that you've retweeted a tweet from the Twitter account of a notorious white supremacist simply because you sell appliances, and he recently talked about how much he loves his new dishwasher.

Some people pay to have artificial followers added to their social media accounts so that they can appear more seasoned and well-known than they actually are. This is usually a mistake. First, fake accounts don't usually comment on your posts, so it's suspicious if you don't have a lot of these followers interacting with you. People don't like posers and if they suspect you've done this, there may be backlash. Also, these followers can clog up your feeds and get in the way of you seeing what's really effective, and who your true audience is so that you can target them more effectively.

For these reasons, most of us in the industry recommend you build your audience authentically and organically.

Get Involved in Online Groups

There's a very successful pair of realtors from south Florida. They don't advertise, yet they have many employees under them who are continually busy taking calls. Their success is due to how active this pair is on their social media and in online groups.

Their methods are very simple. They've joined hobby groups and they interact with them continually.

They take pictures of themselves daily, as they go about their lives. One Saturday they might go fishing together and post photos to their local fishing group. The next day one goes out on his bicycle and posts snaps of his experiences to his bike group and the nature group he's involved with. That night, his partner might be at a fancy restaurant, taking a photo of his favorite dish and posting it in a foodie group.

These local groups see enough of these two realtors that they feel they know them. There is a truism: People buy from the people that they like. So, when it comes time for a potential client to buy or sell a home, these two are the first realtors that come to mind. And if you interact with enough groups, you can create a booming business.

There are some people that might see this as manipulative. However, these two are only involved in groups that reflect their genuine interests. Almost everyone has certain hobbies and passions, and there are groups out there for almost anything.

Handle Trolls With Caution

When you are in the public eye, you will inevitably run across trolls and other detractors.

If someone is lying about you online, or if they're trying to start a fight, take a deep breath. Consider what your reply should be (or if you should reply at all). Remember that it's public and anyone can see it, even if you take it down again immediately. There are many cringeworthy reports of people posting something terrible, regretting it, and removing it within seconds only to realize that someone has already captured a screenshot of it.

I highly recommend *Hug Your Haters*, by Jay Baer. He explains how to handle even the toughest situations. It should be mandatory reading for anyone dealing with customers and he helps you with advice on everything from phone calls to hate-filled reviews online. Especially when it comes to social media, you must always be alert to any new posts about you or your company, and be prepared to act quickly.

Baer emphasizes that "customer service is a spectator sport" online. In other words, many customers and potential customers are paying attention to what is said about you and how you handle it. Overall, Twitter users get a faster response to business complaints than any other channel and most of the "haters" are happy with the response speed they get.

Facebook is more difficult, even though 75% of all social media complaints take place there. It's not like Twitter, because unless the complaint is posted on your company's own FB page, it's possible you might not even see it. That's why it's important to set alerts to let you know when you or your company name is mentioned publicly. How Facebook's latest algorithm changes may affect this is anyone's idea.

However, Google allows you to set alerts for mentions on the internet, and you can also do a daily search on your social media platforms as part of the regular maintenance.

Be Careful What You Say and How You Say it

There are many stories about companies and individuals that thought they were posting something witty only to find out that they offended tons of people. Yes, I know that some people can be oversensitive. But if enough people take offense, you are in a world of hurt. One example is a zoo account that posted this in African American Vernacular English (AAVE) to celebrate a chunky otter:

> "Abby is a thicc girl
> What an absolute unit
> She c h o n k
> Look at the size of this lady
> OH LAWD SHE COMIN
> Another Internetism !"

Obviously this angered many African Americans who felt they were being mocked, and it could be viewed as cultural appropriation. The responses were blistering.

Here's another example of a corporate tone-deaf tweet:

You: why is my balance so low
Bank account: make coffee at home
Bank account: eat the food that's already in the fridge
Bank accouunt: you don't need a cab, it's only three blocks
You: I guess we'll never know
Bank account: seriously?
- Chase Bank

It came across as a wealthy bank lecturing people that their financial woes were all their own fault. A Presidential candidate even waded into it all to scold Chase. The outroar resulted in Chase backpedaling with an apology.

If this makes you nervous, it should. The best scenario is to hire a professional to manage your accounts. But if you can't, then ask yourself what message you're trying to convey. I can guess that Chase was trying to tell people that they should manage their money wisely. However, Chase isn't generally seen as a financial advisor. Chase is a bank. Therefore, Chase's message should have been focusing on what services they offer as a bank. They still could have kept a playful tone, and their message might have looked like this:

You: Why do I feel like I'm just a number at my local bank?
Chase: Hey! Check it out! We've got smiling faces!
Chase: ...and coffee!
Chase: Try us! You'll LOVE us!
You: Guess this is what I have to put up with.
Chase: Seriously? *waving*
#bank #hometown #youarespecial

This last hashtag is an example of a hashtag that isn't trending, but is designed to sum up the message that's being conveyed. Sometimes this type of fun little summary is the ultimate punchline.

Your Business Should Appear on Each Major Social Media Platform

I still would recommend the top three for every business: Facebook, Twitter, and LinkedIn. If your company can produce a lot of visual material (ex. an art gallery or craft store) or is involved in a lot of events, then definitely add Instagram, TikTok, and YouTube to your social media portfolio.

Your Page Headers and Profile Photos Must Be Consistent

"Presenting a brand consistently across all platforms can increase revenue by up to 23%," says *Forbes*.

Each of your social media pages must look as much alike as possible. This is a way to show professionalism and keeps people from getting confused or wondering if they all belong to the same company or individual.

Because each social media platform has a different size header, you will need to have a designer create a header for each platform. If you use the same header for all of them, it will appear stretched in one platform, cut off in another, and so on. Keep your header professional and avoid clutter. A photograph is fine, if it's one you use repeatedly in your messaging.

Likewise, use the same profile photo and make sure it's centered, clear and easy to see. Don't use very small photos or they'll look pixelated and unprofessional. It's best to use your corporate logo as the profile photo if it's a corporate account.

If a professional company like mine is doing your social media management, you can expect them to do this design work as part of the package.

Post Three Times or More Each Week

Content is king! Only post about things that are relevant to you or your company. Obviously you need to avoid content that is negative or could be viewed negatively.

Example: If you make umbrellas, you can post about anything that involves umbrellas, like rainy weather. But when very severe weather occurs, such as hurricanes, don't post that your umbrellas are great in all types of weather. Again, you must be thoughtful about how others will perceive your messages. You don't want to look as if you're being opportunistic.

Example: Say you own a bakery. You can show off a gorgeous wedding cake on Monday, talk about how your brioche pairs well with a cup of robust coffee on Wednesday, and on Friday you can encourage everyone to celebrate the end of the week with one of your famous brownies. You might even post a Marie Antoinette meme ("Let them eat cake!"). However, don't start posting about how you use real butter but your competitor, Cassie's Cupcakes, uses lard, unless you want a nasty public spat to come your way. Those never end well.

ALWAYS INCORPORATE PUBLICITY WINS INTO YOUR SOCIAL MEDIA CAMPAIGN

Whenever you get publicity, make the most of it. Be sure that all publicity mentions are posted across all the platforms at least twice.

TV or Radio Interview Example: You're an author who is about to be interviewed on your local station. You tell everyone on social media that the interview is happening tomorrow at 6 PM on The Chatterbox Show.

On the day of your interview, you tell everyone it's happening today, again with the time and how to tune in.

On the day after your interview, you talk about a highlight and/or post a snippet from the interview with a comment.

Two weeks later, you mention it again and add that you forgot to say this, or wish you'd said that, etc. You can even do a "remember this" post a year later!

At all times you want to use appropriate hashtags. Make sure you know what The Chatterbox Show hashtag is. Is it #TCS? Is it #Chatterbox or #ChatterboxShow? If you're well known enough to drive interest, then also hashtag your name. If you're just beginning to build your brand, I would use hashtags that represent your industry or theme.

Print Interview Example: I've known clients who were interviewed by a major publication, and then find out that the story was killed or shelved. So if the interview is an online/offline print interview, you probably should only mention it after it's been published.

On the day that it's published, put up a link, write something pithy about it.

On the day after, do something similar for anyone that missed the first post. Don't repost it verbatim – mix it up a bit.

Two weeks later, you mention it again (with the link) and add a new thought about it. And, like other publicity opportunities, you can "remember" it months or years later.

This time your appropriate hashtags should include the publication you were in. Again, make sure that you know what set of hashtags that publication uses. Is it #WSJ or #WallStreetJournal, or both? And if you're well known, hashtag your own name. If you're not, use hashtags that represent your industry or theme.

ADVERTISING ON SOCIAL MEDIA PLATFORMS

With the exception of TikTok and YouTube (which rely primarily on video content) all other platform ads are usually static (non-movement). They usually consist of a photo or graphic to capture attention, along with wording that will, hopefully, create click-throughs and purchases. However, we are seeing that viewers are increasingly more responsive to moving forms of advertising. You can always try both and make your own decision by using A/B testing.

IDENTIFYING YOUR AUDIENCE

Determining your audience may be more challenging than you realize. Sometimes you may believe you have the right audience, but find yourself surprised to discover you've targeted the wrong demographic. That absolutely does happen.

The easiest way to discover your target audience is to examine your competition's strategy and see who's responding to *their* social media posts. As you develop your social media campaign, you also can get a better understanding of who your audience truly is.

Also, do some internet research. Look into the type of audience that's ideal for your message or your product by googling your topic and add one or two additional words like "customers," "demographics" or "trends." It's a good idea to do this regularly, because this can change over time. There are demographics for almost everything, but be careful. Don't fall for the sites where you must pay to get statistics and other information about a particular topic.

I think you'll agree that there's not a huge market for lampshades, because they usually come with the lamps we buy. How many of us regularly go lampshade shopping? Not many. So, I decided to make lampshades my test case, in order to demonstrate how easy it is. I googled "lampshade demographics," and immediately skipped the first page, which led to nothing but individual pages of pitches generated by bots. If you went to one of these pages, there was a promise of more to come… if you were willing to spend a small fortune. Don't ever do that.

I then googled "lampshade trends," and I immediately found data on the variety of lampshades that are currently available. Additionally, it took me in the direction of lamp trends. This is an example of how one search might lead to other finds that you didn't expect. After all, if you're a lampshade manufacturer, shouldn't you also know what the latest lamp trends are?

And yet, I was still no wiser about lampshade demographics.

So then I typed in "what type of customers buy lampshades," and I hit paydirt! The third article was *"The Secrets of Shade Sales."* It was full of helpful information. If I can find the data I wanted after only three quick searches, you can do it, too.

However, if you're not seeing the success you expected from your advertising efforts, and you're sure that you're chasing after the right audience for your product, then re-examine your ad design and wording.

AD DESIGN

Vertical Ads

Because people generally hold their phones vertically, it's wise to make sure your ads cater to that. And always double check what your ad looks like on mobile, as well as the web, before you go live with it.

Make Sure You Have the Right Size for the Right Platform

Each platform has different optimal sizing for their ads. The maximum ad image file size for all six is 30MB. Facebook and Instagram currently recommend a design size (for a static, non-moving ad) of 1080x1080 pixels, Twitter is 1200x1200, TikTok is 720x1280, LinkedIn is 1104x736, and YouTube is quite a bit more complicated (see below).

Text Needs to be Short and Simple

The text needs to be in an easy-to-read font such as Arial or Calibri, so that someone skimming past it will still be able to easily register it. Text should never be more than 20% of the entire image space. Keep reworking what you want to say until it fits within these parameters, and save the longer verbiage for the landing page where the customer will be sent to when they click on the ad for more information.

Ads Can be Placed in Multiple Ways on Social Media

Depending on the social media site, you can pay to place your ads in a variety of places, including the news feed, which is usually the most expensive choice with the best results. However, there are additional options, such as at the side of the screen, as an overlay to a video, etc.

Make sure you carefully consider all possibilities when placing an ad, and do some research to see what the most recent success rates are for each option. At this time, I've found that even though the news feed is usually the optimal place, an ad that is off to the side but clearly visible can also be quite effective.

Calls to Action and Enticing Value Propositions

"Call to action is a marketing term for any design to prompt an immediate response or encourage an immediate sale." (Wikipedia)

Examples include "Click here to get 20% off," "This sale for one day only," "Buy 1 Get 1 Free," etc. The most effective ads have some form of a call to action.

Enticing Value Propositions (EVP) are, according to Salescripter, "The value that you deliver can typically impact your clients on three different levels – technical, business, and personal." EVPs aren't as necessary in ads, but if you can work them into an ad, it absolutely can create an additional incentive. An EVP could be a company motto, such as Slack's "Be More Productive at Work with Less Effort."

I once oversaw marketing and publicity for a green cleaning product company. Even though everyone privately admitted those products were less effective than the standard products on the market, they were sold to companies that preferred to use a more environmentally friendly product. Those companies had reasons that were all health-related. For such a target audience, you could simply say something like "Environmentally friendly, no harsh chemicals," or "Easy on the environment, easy on you."

Ultimately, every ad should have a call to action, preferably embedded in the graphic and in the accompanying text. If you have a strong EVP with a short, catchy phrase, try to work that in, too.

VIDEO AND CAROUSEL ADS

A static ad is still very well received. So if your budget isn't large enough for a quality ad with movement, spend your money on creating the best static ad you can. But, because people increasingly prefer moving content, it's often the best choice.

Videos aren't always a good option if you're dealing with a small budget, so an alternative to keep in mind are carousel ads (a series of photos or video snippets). They're known for much higher than average click-through and conversion rates.

No matter what you choose, you're probably not an expert in this area. So, if it's a small project, find an individual that can do this for you. A larger project (such as creating videos of staff members discussing various procedures) should probably go to a larger group that is experienced in doing this type of project.

The maximum video size for any platform currently seems

to be 4GB. However, since both TikTok and YouTube are different, a video that could work well on one might not work on the other. The next two sections are here to help you understand the differences, and how you can use them to your advantage.

With YouTube, whether it's a static graphic or video, the overlay ads (the banner you see embedded at the bottom of the video you're watching) are 728x90 or 480×70. I recommend this second, less-intrusive size, since it's more likely the viewer won't need to click the "x" and remove it because it's interfering with their visual field.

The YouTube display ads (to the right of the video you're watching) should be 300x250 with a maximum video length of 30 seconds.

Skippable ads for YouTube (you can click "skip" after the mandatory 5 seconds you're forced to watch the ad) are 300x600 and supposedly limited to 6 seconds. Although it's wise to keep them to 5 seconds (or not use them at all), I've recently seen some that go far longer than 6 seconds.

YouTube's bumper ads are the mandatory non-skippable 6-second ad that must be viewed prior to the content. These video ads should also be 300x600, with no more than 1KB of content.

I prefer bumper ads over the skippable ones because the viewer feels that less games are being played. He understands he must sit through that entire ad before he gets to view the content he wants. That creates a situation where he has a promised end in sight. According to *The Atlantic's* article How Uncertainty Fuels Anxiety, "Studies have shown…greater nervous-system activation when waiting for an unpredictable shock or unpleasant stimulus, than an expected one." Also, his finger isn't hovering over the "skip" option, concentrating on the countdown to "skip" rather than listening to your message. Most importantly, a bumper ad causes your full content to be seen.

If you'd prefer to create a skippable ad, let that first 5 seconds be strong enough so the viewer may not click "skip."

TikTok Marketing Must Take a Different Approach

The following advice is from our Social Media Director, Miguel Lantigua. Throughout his career, Miguel has worked with over 90 professional brands on content creation, social media marketing and SEO management. He specializes in content creation, which includes social media strategy, graphics, videos, and post-production editing.

Whether as a Team Lead or Sole Producer, Miguel's spent the past 15 years producing content for independent and high level brands such as The North Face, Nike, Fightbox TV, Saradan Films and New Line Cinema on a variety of projects from vlogs to podcast to film trailers. He currently runs an independent music publishing label Elsewhere Playhaus in St Pete, Florida.

Brands may have a tough time competing for eyes in an endless sea of influencers on TikTok, often because these brands make the mistake of falling into the old habit of using platforms as perpetual ad awareness pages.

While corporate adoption of social media has been met with mixed responses, they have been widely accepted (most unironically) by Millenials. However, the demographic for TikTok is predominantly Gen Z. Capturing that same attention from Gen Z proves to be more difficult, with high profile brands such as Gatorade failing to reach the same engagement and followership on TikTok as on Twitter or Facebook, where their followers reach millions.

Like most issues on social media, this is a content-driven one. TikTok has a far more personal feel. Users follow other users and influencers, interacting and collaborating on videos, and this is by design — you can't hide behind an avatar or corporate label. Users also go on TikTok expecting to avoid the same advertisers that can clog up their feeds on Instagram, Facebook, or Twitter, which are platforms struggling to maintain their younger users.

The very thing that makes TikTok appealing has also made it more difficult to advertise: Tiktok has democratized content creation. All you need is a phone, an account and you can start posting immediately. On top of that, both Gen Z and Millennials (the second largest demographic on TikTok) have grown up in an increasingly media-focused world, so they are more discerning about what they spend their time watching. Gen Z, in particular, is very aware of being patronized and resents obvious pandering. As a result, accounts and videos that feature their users are far more successful than ones that push advertising content. The upside is that this is perfect for brands with mascots or spokespeople, as well as those that are not afraid to be creative in a landscape which celebrates imagination over messaging and polish.

It's interesting to see that some brands have been able to establish their own voice and move past the corporate baggage that comes with being a high-profile brand, even without a clear spokesperson or mascot. Since you can scroll past content quickly on TikTok, users must be given something interesting to watch. This presents a challenge, but there are successful companies (such as Underarmour and Food52) that create entertaining and valuable content for their users, rather than bombarding them with ads.

When I first read Miguel's insights, I got so excited that I shared it with journalist Emma Rose, who published some of this in her article Business Experts Share Their Best Advice for TikTok Success *on Idea Rocket.*

A/B TESTING FOR ADS

There is a tremendous amount of material out there about ad design, so I won't dive deeply into tactics. My team is phenomenal at designing the proper ad for the proper medium and target audience, and that's due to their experience. It's very probable this isn't your specialty, so let me repeat that you can hire someone to do it for you, because nothing beats experience.

But say that you're down to two final designs, or your expert has presented you with some choices. What if you can't decide between two different approaches?

That's pretty typical in the industry. We generally know what works, but things can change. Even when you're almost certain you know what's going to work, it never hurts to do some A/B testing to discover how the targeted audience will respond. We use A/B testing regularly. If you're doing your social media campaign, and you've done your homework and you're still undecided, you should conduct your own A/B testing.

A/B testing is when different people see two different versions of something, like an ad on Facebook. It can be used to figure out which version people like better. If enough people prefer ad A, measured by click-through rate, then at some point during the campaign ad B will be removed, and only ad A will continue to be used.

Remember that what works on one platform may not work on another platform. That's why it's also so important to know your audience demographics. Regularly monitor both campaigns (look at them at least once a day). If one particular ad has received a far more enthusiastic response than the other one, it may be time to immediately discontinue the less popular campaign. At that point, run the winning ad only.

CHAPTER 8

WEBSITES AND BLOGS

One of the first companies I started was a website design company. Over the years, as a Marketing and/or Publicity Director, I would either direct a team or do the design myself, as needed. I'm no longer the best website designer, because the industry changes at a rapid pace, but I know what designs work and I stay current on trends.

However, I'm not going to get into all the intricacies of a well-designed website. I *will* caution you to keep it up to date. But I want you to use your publicity effectively in everything you do, so here are a couple of basics to keep in mind:

1. If you haven't created your website yet, don't get too creative with the URL. I've had authors that wanted their URL to be something like thegreatestsage.com and then they're surprised when it's difficult to publicize. The truth is that an URL like that is generic. You know what's usually less generic? Your name.
2. You need a media tab that is kept up to date. When you, your company, or your spokesperson receive publicity, it needs to go on that page along with links to the articles, embedded videos or snippets from interviews. You can also post news stories that are relevant to your message, but not about you directly. However, do this sparingly and be mindful of when they might go out of date and become unnecessary.
3. On the home page, you should consider a scrolling banner that will feature your top publicity hits. Remember that at the very beginning of this book I mentioned that publicity must be ongoing so that you and your message remain fresh? If you take

this to heart, you'll always have material for this banner.

4. If someone clicks on a tab, there'd better be something on that page. I can't tell you how many times I've clicked on a tab only to find that there's only a placeholder there. Remove empty pages immediately. If you want to add it again later when you have data, go for it.

5. Keep the color scheme consistent with your other company colors and logo. It's very jarring to see a discordant website and it can turn people off. And remember that less is more. Don't crowd the viewer with unnecessary words, graphics, or photos.

6. Keep your wording simple (about tenth grade level) unless you absolutely must use bigger words. A website about a rare disease should use college-level diction when necessary, but a website that sells embroidery kits should not.

7. Keep an active blog on your website. It's a great way to keep information current and create SEO data. You may feel that the term "blog" is outdated, so feel free to choose an alternative name. One of my clients has their blog named "articles," but I would caution against this because articles can be culled from other sources. You need original content to show you're unique, as well as give a boost to your SEO ratings. If it's a more intimate-style site, consider options like "Musings," "Thoughts," "Check It Out," etc. If it's a professional site, consider "From Our CEO," "Talking Law," "What's Happening," "You Should Know," etc. Try to keep the title short and sweet.

ONE SITE IS BETTER THAN TOO MANY

I recently ran into someone who'd been talked into paying for multiple websites. One was for her, and one was for a fictional company that was supposed to make her look more important. When she did her interviews, she pointed people to the "company" site, where they could get a copy of her book. And then, years later, the site remained idle and unchanged. Her real site, which had her name in the URL, was never associated with the "company" site and any initial leads were easily lost because they were attached to the fictional company site. The name recognition wasn't there.

Toyota is a brand. I happen to love Toyota products. In fact, I even have one of the sewing machines they manufactured before they manufactured cars. Under the Toyota label, you have a variety of options: Toyota, Camry, and even sewing machines.

Like Toyota, you or your firm is the major brand. Under that brand might be any number of products such as books, perhaps an item you've invented, services you're selling, and more. So, if you're the primary force behind all of this, you should create your website in your name, and then these various items can each have their own tab or be listed together on a single page on your site.

Let's say that Ken Young is an inventor that usually sells his inventions to various corporations. His site could be KenYoung.com with a tab that takes you to a page displaying each item he's invented, plus another tab for his bio, as well as a tab for his blog titled "What's Next," or "Ken's Notebook."

However, if Ken chooses to sell each of those inventions himself, he should consider creating a separate URL for each product. His inventions page should have a link to each product URL and each product URL should have a link leading back to KenYoung.com. Generally, if you're an author, you do *not* need an individual site for each book you've written. Individual sites should be for products or organizations.

What if you don't own the company that you work for, but you have your own website? Feel free to mention where you work, but you don't have to link to their site and you shouldn't, unless it benefits you in some way.

BLOG POSTS

Many years ago, I had a blog that covered local politics and events. It was named one of the top blogs in the Tampa Bay area by both major newspapers at the time. Eventually, I found it too onerous to continue with the blog, but I learned a great deal, and I continue to stay on top of the latest recommendations for successful blogs.

At one time, it was common wisdom that blog posts should be short and to the point, or the readers would get bored and move on. In fact, we all kept getting bombarded with the fact that the average attention span seems to be getting smaller!

However, Semrush.com put out an in-depth analysis in February 2021. They noted that blog "…long-form content generates eight times more page views, three times more social media shares, and nine times more leads than short-form content. 75% of people prefer reading articles under 1,000 words. While shorter articles are preferred, longer articles do better in rankings and website visits because they are more comprehensive. Blogs that earn over $50,000 per year say their most popular posts are 2,424 words long."

Your blog should be a great place to get content for your own marketing and publicity projects. Posts can be reworked into a media pitch, and segments can be used in marketing materials and publications. Each time a post is published, a link to that post should be on every one of your social media platforms.

Keeping your blog fresh and full of interesting material shows everyone that your company is current, and gives you an aura of authority. And "82% of consumers feel more positive about a brand after reading customized content." (Demand Metric)

Obviously blogging can be an exhausting and time-consuming chore. That's why I'd recommend you consider hiring one or more writers (or a publicist or marketing firm) to regularly create blog content. However, it's possible to do your own blogging and search engine optimization.

SEO (SEARCH ENGINE OPTIMIZATION)

Seth Czerepak is an author, copywriter, and Harvard Certified Neuroscientist and also holds degrees in philosophy, music theory, and developmental psychology. Since 2009, Seth has ghostwritten and edited hundreds of books on the topics of leadership, cognitive behavior therapy, entrepreneurship, and critical thinking. Seth's professional experience includes 15,000 hours of direct response copywriting for websites and other projects. In particular, two areas of expertise include SEO concepts and website design. I asked him to contribute to this portion.

Three Evergreen Rules for Effective SEO

SEO stands for Search Engine Optimization. In my opinion, this label is misleading and causes many people to fail at SEO. If I had to create one timeless principle for effective SEO it would be this:

"SEO is about optimizing your website content for people, not search algorithms."

If people like your website content, search engines will like your website content too. It's that simple. Most SEO failures are the result of people either not understanding this principle or trying to get around it.

Since 2008, I have witnessed countless webmasters, marketers, and businesses (small and large) struggle to secure and to keep solid search engine rankings. I've also seen a handful of smart and diligent people turn their website into an evergreen source of high-quality inbound leads.

Without question, the most striking difference between those who succeed at SEO, and those who fail, boils down to this simple idea: SEO is about optimizing your website for people, not search algorithms.

I still remember the 2011 "Panda Update" when hundreds of websites (including some big-name brands) watched their web traffic disappear within hours. For two years prior, I had been warning people to stop trying to fool search engines with shady SEO techniques that would soon prove irrelevant and detrimental to their rankings.

I didn't need a crystal ball to tell me why this was true or what Google was about to do with their next update. I simply knew that Google was interested in ranking websites that were optimized for users, and that their algorithms would be continually refined to meet that goal.

That said, I know you're looking for specific advice on how to put this principle into practice.

The following three rules are guaranteed to work no matter what Google (or any search engine) does in the future. They contain the simplest most trustworthy strategies for making your website content more interesting, engaging, and trustworthy to human users.

#1: Structure is Everything

The most common problem I run into with new clients is poor website structure. To use a metaphor, your website's pages (including your blogs) need to be structured like a tree. Imagine your homepage as the trunk, your cornerstone pages (about us, and service or product pages) as the primary branches, and your blog articles as the smaller branches. Every branch represents a keyword you're trying to rank for.

Your home page keyword should represent the primary category for ALL content on your website. It should also represent a keyword that's as relevant as possible to the people searching for your product or service.

For example, let's assume you're doing SEO for a Dog Training Service Company website. Here's an example of the keywords your cornerstone pages should be optimized for.

Homepage: Dog Training Services
About Page: Dog Training Company
Service Page:
1. Dog Obedience Training Services
2. Guide Dog Training Services
3. Diabetes Alert Dog Training Services
4. Mobility Assistance Dog Training
5. Psychiatric Service Dog Training

Notice how all your cornerstone pages branch off from your primary keyword. Each of these pages should contain a contextual link back to the home page using the link text "Dog Training Services." This will tell search engines that your homepage contains the content most relevant to that keyword. For the same reason, your service pages should contain one contextual link back to your "about" page, using the link text "Dog Training Company."

You should never have two pages on your website optimized for the same keyword or keywords that are too similar to one another. This will confuse readers, and search engines, and hurt your rankings. Also, never try to "straddle" two primary categories and hope to rank for both at the same time. As the saying goes "if you chase two rabbits, you'll lose them both." Likewise, if you try to rank for two keyword categories your website won't rank well for either. In other words, if you want to branch out and start selling products (dog treats, leashes, crates, etc), you need to build a new website and optimize it around a general category like "Buy Dog Products Online."

Each of your cornerstone pages should have between 750 and 1,000 words, and the content should not be fluff. If you don't know what to write about, hire a professional writer, and be prepared to pay them well. Writers who work for slave wages create lousy content, and your rankings will suffer for it.

That's all there is to creating your cornerstone website content. If you apply the next two rules wisely, you won't have to worry about overhauling the content for your cornerstone pages, or even building links.

#2: Your Monthly Content Strategy

Once your cornerstone pages are done, the rest of your SEO strategy will involve creating and publishing high-quality blog articles that will achieve two goals:

1. Rank well for their own keywords
2. Boost rankings for your cornerstone pages

This second rule is simple to apply, but commonly misunderstood or even neglected. Every blog article you write should be a subcategory to one of your cornerstone pages. Continuing with our Dog Training example, the content categories for your blog should be based on the keywords of your service pages:

Blog Article Categories:
1. Dog Obedience Training
2. Guide Dog Training
3. Diabetes Alert Dog Training
4. Mobility Assistance Dog Training
5. Psychiatric Service Dog Training

Let's use your "Diabetes Alert Dog Training" category as an example. Here are three blog articles you might write to support this category (the keywords are in bold type):
1. Best **Diabetes Alert Dog Breeds**

2. Heartwarming **Diabetes Alert Dog Stories**
3. Five Proven **Diabetes Alert Dog Benefits**

Each one of these blogs should contain two contextual links. The first contextual link should lead back to your home page using the keyword "Dog Training Company" as the link text. Your second contextual link should lead to your Diabetes Alert Dog Training page using the keyword "Diabetes Alert Dog Training" as the link text.

Use this linking strategy EVERY time you create a new blog article for your website. This way, if your blog articles rank well, the links leading back to your cornerstone pages will add "SEO juice" to those pages as well. This is called your "internal linking strategy," and it's super important to your long-term SEO success.

Just make sure you don't overdo your internal linking. I suggest limiting your internal links to one link every five hundred words. You can usually create your home page link by including something like this in the introduction to all your blog articles (the bold portion is where the link would be inserted):

*"This article is brought to you by ACME Dog Training, who has been providing professional **dog training services** to Tampa, Florida for thirty years."*

Remember, however, the two rules we talked about a moment ago:

1. Make sure that all your blog articles represent "branches" of the keyword categories defined in your cornerstone pages.
2. As with your cornerstone pages, you should never create two blog articles that are based on the same, or similar keywords.

#3: Three Rules of Great Content

If you've read any articles about how to do SEO, you're probably sick of this kind of generic advice:

"Write great content!"
"Write content that's engaging!"
"Make your content relevant!"

This advice is about as helpful as telling someone who can barely change the oil on their car to rebuild their own transmission. Over the past ten years, I've been conducting detailed surveys (polling real web users) on what kind of content they want to read. Based on this data, I've narrowed my list down to three things:

1. Author Credibility

The person who writes your blog articles needs to be an expert in the article topic. Not a self-proclaimed expert. God knows that the internet is crawling with those already. If I had to predict what will become the ace in the hole for the future of SEO, it would be this.

Ideally, you want someone with a formal education or certification on your topic to be the author of your blog articles. If this isn't possible, find someone who has a credible published reputation (online) for writing on your topic.

Do *not* ignore this rule and assume you can make up for it by doing well with the other rules below. Web users are tired of anonymity and looking for authentic content written by credible authors and search engines are already creating ways to weed out imposters. I predict that search engines will become even more diligent about this in the near future, and that a lot of imposter content will disappear from the search engine rankings. It's not a matter of *if* this will happen, it's a matter of *when*. So, you're better off getting ahead of the game now.

2. Content Depth and Detail

Your articles should be no shorter than three thousand words, and ideally up to ten or even twenty thousand words. If this sounds overwhelming, it's probably because you've been told that you have to publish every week or every two weeks. This is an outdated SEO myth that should have died around 2011.

I've seen companies get remarkable results by publishing one rock solid, detailed article every month or even four times a year. Your articles should also be easy to scan and should include multiple forms of media (audio, video, images, infographics). Most importantly, again they should contain no fluff. This will mean more time spent on research and planning, which is one reason I advise people not to pay their writers by word count.

Writers who are experts in their topics don't usually charge by word count anyway. They charge for the value and insight they bring to your content. This is the mindsight you need to have when hiring a content writer.

3. Thought Leadership

By "thought leadership," I mean that your blog articles should be a source of highly relevant data, research, and statistics related to your industry. No matter what industry you're in, I guarantee you there's someone gathering and publishing data about your industry, your product/service type, or your target market. I'm advising you to become this person so that people will link to *your* blog articles when writing theirs.

There are multiple ways to do this, but the easiest is to create your own surveys and buy responses using a service like

SurveyMonkey. This will cost money for each survey response, but if you're gathering good and interesting data with your surveys, the return on investment will be more than worth it.

Sure, you can link to data, research, and statistics published by someone else. But if you want to stand head and shoulders above all the other content publishers in your industry, why not get those people linking to you instead? The smartest way to build organic backlinks (the only kind that search engines trust these days) is to entice other publishers to link to your content to verify their own claims.

Final Thoughts

In closing, let me debunk an outdated myth about SEO and backlinks. Some SEO enthusiasts cite statistics about the highest-ranking websites also having the most backlinks. While this is statistically true, it's highly misleading.

Websites with great content naturally attract backlinks for the same reason they rank well in search engines. In other words, backlinks and high rankings go together because great content attracts both. To assume that backlinks *cause* high rankings is a dangerous mistake to make.

I know this can be frustrating if you've been creating content for a long time and people aren't linking to it. You might be tempted to wade into the gurgling cesspool of "Blackhat" SEO practices by building backlinks artificially or paying someone to do it. I assure you that if you do, any rankings will be short lived, and you'll run a high risk of being shadow banned or even blacklisted by search engines.

One undeniable rule of SEO is that shortcuts end up being dead ends. You might get away with it for a time, but at some point, search engines will figure out what you're doing. You'll then realize that instead of building links, you should have been creating content that will naturally attract them.

Apply the three rules we just discussed and be persistent. Remember that SEO is about optimizing your website content for people, and your results will take care of themselves.

This concludes Seth's portion. But I have something to add. Most of us had worked with each other in a prior company, before we formed our own organization. However, I had run across Seth online a couple of years before. I was immediately impressed with him, and so I recommended him to one client as an editor. In turn, she was so impressed that she hired him to help author one of her books. After that, I recommended him again to another client, and the same thing happened. Seth has now ghostwritten or edited books for many of my clients. One of our clients says he's her "security blanket." Obviously it's no surprise that I asked him to join the team.

CHAPTER 9

HOW TO BUILD
OR HIRE A GREAT TEAM

Perhaps you've tried the techniques in this book, but you just can't seem to get the coverage you deserve. Or perhaps you don't want to be bothered juggling all of this. You want to hire a firm to do it for you. Ultimately, this book was designed to give you the information you need to make the proper evaluations and ask the right questions. Here are some additional things to consider.

WHAT IF I HAVE A LIMITED BUDGET?

I totally get that. Who doesn't have a limited budget, right?

There's a young millionaire who told me he doesn't like being labeled a millionaire because he has few liquid assets. In fact, he still makes himself lunches that he takes to work every day. His money has all been reinvested in his businesses and not in himself.

Businesses can be money pits! You invest everything you've got in them, and rent and payroll and utilities and all the other bills are still coming in every month. It's nerve-wracking. However, it's a sad truth that when a company is struggling, they often cut their marketing and publicity efforts first. But these efforts are the very thing their company requires to stay afloat.

DON'T BE CHEAP, BUT DON'T OVERSPEND

Remember that you often get what you pay for, so be cautious. There are times you can get the exact same services from a hungry, smaller firm than from their larger competition.

But, if a company is a recent start-up, it may not have the track record to prove that they can do what other companies do. However, that's also a great opportunity to get a good deal on their services before they take off and their rates rise. If you're considering a relatively new firm, examine the individuals in that firm, and ask what their experience in the past has been with clients just like you. Look at their customer reviews from former positions.

For more established firms, look at the company structure and ask questions. Does the head of the company still work there or is he just a figurehead that isn't involved in the daily business? Look at the LinkedIn profiles of the people that will be running your campaign. Do they have legitimate experience? Will you be handed off to a junior staff member after you start?

At the extreme end of the spectrum are companies that charge far more than they should. I know a company whose CEO has proclaimed to everyone in the firm that the company policy is to overprice their goods and services. He believes that if you charge more, value is automatically inferred, and it fools suckers into parting with their hard-earned money. This comic naivete comes from an outdated sales technique that may have worked at one time, but current shoppers are more savvy, and you should be savvy, too. Just because someone is charging more doesn't mean that it's worth more.

On the other end of the spectrum is the cheap option of a one-man-band. Sometimes it's tempting to hire one person, in-house, to do all your marketing and publicity efforts. But no one can be an expert in every area, and it's amazing how many changes continuously occur in publicity and marketing. So though one person may appear to be a bargain, they will always be limited in scope. A single expert with a good resume can oversee campaigns, and direct teams, but they can't effectively do it all.

BEWARE THE HAS-BEENS AND CON ARTISTS

There are many qualified, helpful consultants that are a great help to their clients. However, there's a certain type of self-styled consultant who poses as an expert in the field, when they're not even qualified to advise a rat how to eat cheese.

At one time they may even have been an expert, but that time is long gone. Their website looks like it was made fifteen to twenty years ago, because it probably was. They claim they have a number of successful clients, quote old texts and drop famous names from days-gone-by which might impress a potential client, but an expert will see right through them.

Referring to this type, one of my colleagues said, wryly, "Those who can... do. Those who can't... become consultants."

I have personally known some that don't seem to know how to get out of their own way. Instead of bothering to stay up to date, these people simply work twice as hard to justify bad advice and decisions. Sometimes their motive is to charge you a lot of money and then learn on your dime. Their motto is "fake it 'til you make it."

Let me tell you about a recent encounter I had with one of these types.

I had a client (we'll call him Dan) that hired The Reps to do his publicity campaign. A couple of months later, he hired one of these supposed experts (we'll call him Tony) as his marketing manager because Tony convinced him that he needed additional marketing. As you know by now, the two are very complementary to each other, so it seemed like a good investment to Dan. But, we all soon discovered that Tony was the wrong type of consultant.

To justify their existence, people like this are motivated to find fault with any processes in place so that they can be the hero in the client's eyes. So, Dan asked me to chat with Tony.

Even before our call, Tony sent an email demanding we share everything with him, including proprietary information. Although I refused to share the proprietary info, I guardedly agreed to share our overall attempts and results, and we scheduled the phone call.

Our call went on for 45 minutes. Tony started his shock-and-awe attempt with the usual name-dropping but, as expected, the names were outdated and irrelevant. Tony immediately informed me that he was going to be overseeing Dan's marketing campaign, but generally showed that he had no idea about publicity or marketing in the modern era. He wanted help understanding how the publicity campaign could be best utilized, and I helpfully shared a great deal of advice with him.

During that call, Tony played an old game that many of us know as "Stump the Chump." Stump the Chump is when someone tries to establish superiority by throwing questions at you which are designed to stump you. The goal is to create enough confusion or defensiveness that you drop your guard and give them something that they want. Sometimes, all they want is dominance. In sales, customers might play Stump the Chump to test you and see if you really know what you're talking about. In this case, Tony was obviously hoping to get access to valuable information that he could use. And, I got the very strong impression that he also wanted to establish dominance.

I continued to feel uneasy after that initial call, and I couldn't seem to shake that feeling. With my first sip of morning coffee the next day, I developed a growing conviction that Tony had been pumping me for information so he could take credit for it. I realized that I hadn't done a follow-up summary email of the suggestions I'd made. I immediately created a very detailed memo, and sent it to both Tony and Dan before that first cup was even finished.

Tony never replied to that initial email, which let me know two things. The underlying hostility that I'd sensed from him was real, and I had proven to myself that he was intending to use my information to create a marketing strategy for Dan. The summary from me had put a stop to that, and Tony wasn't happy.

I followed up with a phone call to Dan, who initially said that he was very confused by Tony's claim to be in charge of his marketing campaign, as he had only chosen Tony for some basic guidance. Soon, however, Tony did end up convincing Dan to let him run the marketing campaign.

Next, Tony began a long-running passive-aggressive feud. He started by attempting to do an end-run around me to contact my employees directly for information. The first time I simply told him that this was unacceptable. By the second time, I was more blunt and told him officially, via email, that I would not tolerate it.

Tony continued to get in the way, and our team was growing frustrated. Tony would regularly request calls with us about various issues. Each time I would send out an invite for everyone that was needed, and we'd assemble on Google Meet.

One day Tony did something so completely unethical that I had to alert Dan to it. Dan confronted Tony, who asked for another group meeting.

When the meeting time was agreed upon, I sent another Google Meet invite to everyone, as usual. Suddenly realizing that I had mistakenly set the meeting for a full 1 ½ hours, I quickly amended it to only thirty minutes and re-sent the invitation.

Just before the meeting, with almost no notice, Tony sent out a group email saying that I'd confused him with this change. He explained that his confusion was so great that he suddenly couldn't figure out how to join us on Google Meet. Instead, he asked us to join him on his private Zoom channel. I discussed it with my Social Media Director, Miguel. We agreed it was very odd, but we also felt there was no good reason to refuse, so we joined Tony's Zoom call.

We waited a few minutes and when Tony finally let us in, it became immediately obvious that he'd deliberately kept us waiting as he chatted with Dan. He admitted us into the call just as Dan was mid-sentence from an apparently ongoing discussion.

It was also immediately obvious that Tony was attempting to secretly record us, and had been recording Dan against his knowledge. It's illegal to record anyone without their consent in Florida (where we're based) and also where Tony and Dan live. We firmly told him we would *not* give our consent and Tony had to immediately stop recording us. Dan was shocked.

Although irritating, we continued with the meeting, which was filled with Tony creating excuses and some downright lies to explain away his behavior. As Tony continued, we were forced to refute and disagree with his claims. I just hate it when someone puts you in that type of scenario, don't you? I take no pleasure in proving that someone is wrong, and only do so reluctantly.

After that Zoom call, I decided that I'd had enough. I sent Dan an email stating that we would no longer deal with Tony, and that any further information requests would have to come through Dan.

Of course I empathized with Dan! He was put in an unfortunate situation. After all, he'd already invested in Tony. It's a horrible feeling to suddenly realize that you've fallen prey to someone who doesn't have your best interests at heart. I'm sure that almost everyone has experienced this at least once in their lifetime. I certainly have.

So, to make it easier for Dan to part ways with Tony, I told him that I'd be happy to consult with him on any further choices he needed to make and, if we didn't know the answer to a question, we'd find someone who did.

That uncomfortable conclusion brings us to an important question. How do you avoid this type of con artist?

If you're not savvy in this area, ask people that stay current to evaluate him and his portfolio. If in doubt, consult a Millennial in that field. Most Millennials, like Miguel, grew up on the internet and have developed a good instinct for what's genuine.

By the end, Tony had most definitely proven himself to be highly corrupt. If I'd been Tony, I would have been mortified. During that last meeting, Tony persistently kept a brave face and struggled along with his narrative, while Miguel was primarily the one who patiently dismantled each claim.

Right after that Zoom meeting, Miguel called me, laughing. "YEAH," he enthused. "Teach *him* to try to take on a Millennial!"

COMPARE APPLES TO APPLES

Some companies make guarantees that sound great, until you discover that *their* measures of success really aren't *your* measures. And sometimes you think two companies are offering the same service, but they're not. It's easy to make the mistake of thinking all companies' plans are the same. Be sure that you're clear about what type of service you're getting.

For example, there are firms that can guarantee they'll place you in all the top publications but their clients are placed in advertisements that look like news stories in those publications. You've seen that type of advertisement. It's called an advertorial. That's not publicity. That's marketing. And although marketing is important, it's also important to understand that this form of marketing disguises itself as publicity, when it needs to be in the marketing category.

Another example is talk radio and podcasts. My firm books our clients on genuine radio shows in the top markets, and on podcasts with large audiences. But I know of another firm that tells people they'll book them on a lot of shows, and then they're booked on small time, no-name shows as filler for time slots when no one is tuning in. If no one hears your message, is it worth it?

Some firms offer packages that are supposed to be all-inclusive at a high retainer fee and steep monthly rates. When you examine what their package includes, you may discover that there are a lot of needless items that you can do without. Our firm has an a la carte menu, so you can choose where you want to target your publicity dollars. We found that clients love this model. You don't go to a grocery store and buy a package that forces you to get stuff you don't want, and you shouldn't feel like you have to do that in publicity, either.

Listen for dishonesty. If they promise something that sounds too good to be true, it probably is.

For example, when I talk to clients, I tell them if they're not a good fit for a particular type of media. In fact, I recently had to tell a client that he wasn't ready for TV appearances. When he challenged this, I verified that he wasn't ready for TV by consulting with a colleague who's a former TV producer. He was disappointed, because another firm had just told him that they could guarantee to get him on some of the top TV shows (for a high fee). I knew that firm and could say, with great certainty, that this was impossible for them. So he went with me, because he knew I was telling him the truth, and therefore he could trust me.

EXAMINE CONTRACTS

Whether you hire a large or small firm, make sure that you examine the contract carefully. Look for hidden costs, and don't settle for a simple monthly fee without details about what will be done each month. Make sure the contract matches what you've been verbally told.

HOW TO MAKE THE BEST USE OF YOUR TEAMS

Too often companies have the gift of a brilliant publicity and/or marketing team but immediately set out to micromanage and hobble them. Due to mismanagement, they're left with substandard and feeble attempts. Instead of analyzing what went wrong, the blame is then laid squarely on the people that really had nothing to do with the failures. I've seen this too often.

You can't ask a ditch digger to effectively dig a ditch with a teaspoon and you can't ask a team to do their job if you continually get in the way or don't give them the right data and materials. I once worked for a company that was so paranoid that they kept major, necessary information from the marketing team. When the information was finally "declassified," they forgot to inform the marketing team, and then they wondered why the product designs were delayed. The team was waiting on information that never came.

It's also dangerous to the health of your business to discourage brainstorming and creative input by others. If a business is to grow, then growing pains are inevitable and stepping outside of a comfort zone is not just desirable, but necessary. If you tell your teams exactly what you want done, but discourage their input, they become no more than an advanced computer program executing your limited vision.

You see, someone who has made marketing or publicity their livelihood was attracted to it for a certain reason. They're a curious mix of statistician, psychologist, business professional, and artist. This is not the average individual. If they're stifled or not listened to, this type of person will eventually grow frustrated in the job and look elsewhere, or grow passive, essentially giving up. Neither option is good for the businesses they work for.

Likewise, firms also need to be given flexibility in their designs and concepts. I've had clients argue with my employees about how a particular ad should look. They'll insist on, for example, a particular typeface that is known to create negative impressions (such as Papyrus). It's hard for them to understand that even if *they* like the look of that typeface, it's not appropriate for their ad.

I've also had clients tell me that they are certain their message is perfect for a particular medium, such as TV, when it absolutely is not. Those of us who are immersed in the industry are fully aware of where a message should be delivered, and how it should be presented.

Of course, to trust blindly is foolish. But, you can always ask for justification. A good team will have reasons and research behind their recommendations. Publicity and marketing professionals aren't perfect either, and not all ideas are good ideas. But here's how you can utilize your teams to their fullest.

1. Periodically look over their CVs, LinkedIn profiles, or company portfolios, and take time to catch up on their latest successes. This will help you to familiarize yourself with their strengths and weaknesses. You may find something there that you overlooked before and realize that you desperately need right now.
2. Understand what they were hired for and tap into it. Take the opportunity to step away and be grateful that you are dealing with one less burden. Micromanagement is exhausting.
3. If they're an in-house team, consider investing in ongoing training for them. If you're an accountant, you must stay up on all the latest tax codes and changes. If you're a surgeon, you must stay up to date on the latest techniques. Your team also will benefit from ongoing training, but don't presume to know best. Ask them to tell you what they want to learn and how it could benefit your business if you invest in it.
4. Instead of deciding how you wish to market or publicize something, go to your team and set the problem in front of them.

Ask them to give you some options, and give them a reasonable deadline. Discuss their ideas with experts and people in similar industries that you respect, and get their opinions.

Although it's tempting to play God, resist that temptation and allow others to weigh in. Take the risk to step outside of your comfort zone. Trust the team that you hired, or fire them immediately and find people you can trust. There is no middle ground.

HERE'S HOW ONE CLIENT RUINED HIS OWN INVESTMENT

Commercials sell products. Infomercials give information and that can be a type of crossover product (both marketing and publicity). I've been involved in creating both. Both have value. Infomercials are not overtly asking for money, so they are a great way to build public confidence in your product or message.

This is probably not something you should do on your own. As you know, no one is an expert in all things. You'll often get better results if you trust the people that do it every day. So, when a client hired us to create three infomercials and one commercial, we assumed he understood that we knew what we were doing.

Almost immediately, there were red flags. Virtually as soon as the ink on the contract had dried, he told me that he knew exactly what he wanted. He had overseen some successful videos in the far distant past that had been successful, and this gave him a false confidence. First, those videos had been made decades before. Second, they were made for an industry that was vastly different from the company he currently wanted to promote. But the biggest problem of all was that he didn't believe that this disqualified him from micromanaging the scripts.

We went through numerous edits of the scripts. At first, he insisted on long gab-filled infomercials that were ten minutes long, and he didn't want to hear any disagreements. Many edits and ibuprofens later, they'd evolved into two-minute scripts that I could pass on to the spokesmodels who had to memorize them. The client agreed that it would be best to give the spokesmodels the option to alter the scripts a little to suit their style, in order to sound genuine.

At that point, I believed we were over the biggest hurdle. I moved ahead to book a studio for 2 days, arranged to fly in a particular model he was dead-set on, and I also hired two additional models, a makeup artist, a photographer, a videographer, a video editor, and more. I ran over the lines with the spokesmodels, and we discussed tone and gestures.

Everything was going great, until the client decided to fly in and then proceeded, at the last minute, to interfere in everything from the script to the models to even the way that they spoke.

On the morning of the shoot, as we were still taking our first slug of coffee, he suddenly decided that the spokesmodels had to be forced to read their scripts verbatim, directly from the teleprompter. Up until then, the teleprompter was only going to be used as a prompt. This immediately changed the tone of the infomercials from a cozy, casual appeal to a very artificial delivery. He was a Boomer, and he expected them to sound like Boomers. However, two were Gen Z, one was a very hip Gen X, and none of them had been prepared to sound like a 1960s cigarette commercial.

The client would regularly interrupt a take, make a minor change, and ask them to start all over. Other times, he would arbitrarily declare that they needed to take a breath for every comma, or emphasize a word that didn't need emphasizing. The models grew increasingly jumpy and he grew more irritable.

At one point, he began to angrily berate a spokesmodel. It was unreasonable, and I had to interrupt his tirade to hand her a bottle of water, and stand in between them as she took a deep breath. It pushed everyone closer to the edge and things went from bad to worse.

An additional complication was that entire sets had to be changed, because he'd capriciously decided he didn't like the furniture and props we'd chosen. So, this resulted in a mad dash between sets, while he stalked about, searching for pieces of furniture throughout the adjacent warehouse. We scrambled to cater to his whims, because we had only asked for half of the payment up front. We were trapped in a situation we felt we couldn't easily walk away from. Hindsight is 20/20, of course, but I now realize we should have walked away, regardless.

After a highly stressful day, we finished up. Even then, he went against our recommendations to take the time to view the takes, and insisted we were finished. We had the studio booked for the next day so that we could (if necessary) correct any problems, but, "it's all good," he declared breezily. He just wanted to fly back out.

Can you guess what happened next?

When he saw the final product, he complained that the models weren't always looking into the camera, and their delivery was stiff. We knew that, and he'd been warned that if they were forced to read it directly from the teleprompter it would look unnatural. He just hadn't felt our input was important.

Other complaints were also issues that could have been dealt with if he hadn't been there, constantly tripping everyone up and changing the script repeatedly. And, because he couldn't understand how YouTube videos worked, we spent even more valuable time explaining that some of his ideas simply weren't feasible. His habit of not listening and talking over us caused him to not be able to comprehend even the simplest explanations.

It was a nightmare, and my Social Media Director was about to have a nervous collapse by the time it was done.

We were happy to say goodbye to that client. We both had made mistakes. My mistake was allowing him to interfere.

I should have immediately cancelled the contract and refunded any money that hadn't been spent.

And because our client kept interfering in a process he really didn't understand, he was never satisfied with the product *because* he had been deeply involved in the creation of it.

Don't be that guy. Don't be stubbornly blind or prejudiced.

A good team will collaborate with you. A good team will listen to you. But you must do the same thing.

When you find a reputable firm, let them guide the process. Neither you nor your other employees should have much to say about it outside of what your basic goals and parameters are. Be open-minded enough to realize that people other than you know what they're doing.

You're the captain of the ship. You can steer the ship, but you aren't the ship's engineer. Ask questions, but stay out of the minutiae. You have better things to do.

CHAPTER 10

SELLING

WHAT ARE SALES?

Nah, I'm just kidding. If you don't know what sales are, you're in the wrong place, anyway.

I do want to point out that sales are not only about closing deals, but also should involve connecting with people and building relationships. Oh yes, salespeople must still close deals! But a quality salesperson will do the work to genuinely connect with the client and still ask for the investment.

There are some exceptions, and I'll touch on those later. But even then, a foundation of trust must be built for the potential client to move forward with a sale. And you can help your sales team by creating that trust in advance, through publicity and marketing efforts which give you that stamp of authority. This can shorten the sales cycle, because the customer already has a level of comfort in the company and product.

Perhaps *you* are the only person selling. If you're an author or a sole proprietor, you're selling every time you try to convince someone to buy your product, whether it's a book or a widget. But even if you're the only one selling, this is for you.

GOOD SALESPEOPLE ENHANCE YOUR EFFORTS

Perhaps people are reading about your CEO in Fortune. Say that people are seeing your ads. Maybe they're opening your emails, but instead of pushing the embedded button that takes them to an assigned landing page, they simply call in to speak with a salesperson. How do you know which campaign led them to call your company?

This is why your salespeople must always ask, "How did you hear about us?" Make it mandatory for them to collect and pass this information on to the marketing department.

A salesperson can jot down where these various clients come from and report the totals to the marketing department on a regular basis. Don't expect that to be accurate, however. Ideally, a salesperson must input that information into the company CRM (customer relationship management database) every time a new client calls in.

Stop laughing.

OK, yeah. Salespeople don't always feel that they have the time to do this. Their natural goal is to move on to the next client as quickly as possible. Instead of hating them for this, understand that this hunter mentality is what you want and need in a good salesperson. A good hunter doesn't take the time to tidy up after a kill. Imagine a magnificent lioness pausing after killing a gazelle to use a napkin and do the dishes.

However, you still need to force these hunters into a semi-civilized co-existence with your marketing department. Your bottom line depends on this.

One easy way to force your sales team to cough up the critical data is to create a system where they can't proceed without providing it. Sometimes that means that a CRM can't progress another step until they click on how the lead came to them. Since salespeople are often your best and brightest, they can easily find a workaround. They may click anything in their rush to move on, or they may also get excited by a lead and forget to ask that lead where they heard about your company. Then what?

HOW TO HERD THE HUNTER

In an ideal situation, the best sales managers rely heavily on patience and a strict preference for truth-telling. If a manager is forgiving and open, employees are more likely to be that way, also. Let your salespeople know that you will not punish the truth, but you will most definitely punish concealment of it. Allow them to come to you when mistakes are made. This keeps them from being the roadblock, and gives you the chance to fix problems before they grow worse.

There are obvious exceptions. If a salesperson says or does something that is truly unethical or illegal, you may be forced to take more drastic steps. But in most cases, salespeople want to keep their jobs, and it's in your best interest to help them do that.

The best salespeople are clever hunters who hunt for both themselves and the tribe they represent. The more they feel invested in the tribe, the better the chances are that they'll thrive and stay in place. You can help them remain loyal if you keep a healthy work environment.

UNETHICAL SELLING

When I'm in a crowd, and I mention Jordan Belfort, there is always at least one salesperson who enthusiastically endorses him. In fact, I once worked at a highly dysfunctional company that made his book, *The Way of the Wolf,* mandatory reading. Because many people revere Jordan Belfort as a great sales guru, it's important to discuss his advice.

At one time or another, we've all been told "consider the source." Although he was made glamorous by Leonardo DiCaprio's portrayal, the reality is that Belfort is a convicted felon. This isn't some extraordinary miscarriage of justice. It's well-earned. Surely someone who is so cutthroat can take down not only himself and his colleagues, but can destroy entire companies, as well.

Let's start with the least dangerous advice Belfort gives when he recommends that you purchase his aromatherapy oils, which supposedly help set the mood and will increase your sales. This obvious pitch to sell you something that does no more than give off a smell is pitiful. And it's not the only thing that smells.

He is horrifically abusive to his subordinates, and brags about it. Yet, fear has repeatedly been proven to be an ineffective motivator. Although it's important to communicate clearly to your employees about their performance, it should never be done sadistically.

In Leah Fessler's report "Good managers give constructive criticism—but truly masterful leaders offer constructive praise," she writes:

"A 2015 Gallup survey found that 67% of employees whose managers communicated their strengths were fully engaged in their work, as compared to 31% of employees whose managers only communicated their weaknesses. One study found that high-performing teams receive nearly six times more positive feedback than less effective teams—evidence that positive reinforcement really does help the bottom line."

Some other glaring issues that need to be examined:

Belfort loves flashing statistics around without any sourcing. Why provide genuine facts when you can just make something up? But in an age when critical thought is in short supply, his fans have never thought to question where he gets his supposed "facts."

He also touts the highly controversial, dodgy theory of NLP (neuro linguistic programming) as a way to con your mark into buying from you. NLP is manipulation, for good or evil, that supposedly works if the practitioner employs a mixture of techniques. Think of it as a type of supposed hypnosis.

Dr. Rob Yeung is "...a performance psychologist, business coach, keynote speaker and TV presenter who helps people to achieve their goals." Additionally, he's the author of over 20 bestselling books. On his website, he has an entire section devoted to NLP, titled "Why should you be wary about NLP?"

Dr. Yeung writes that certified experts are very unimpressed. In one example, from a survey in 2006, "NLP was rated at 3.87. In fact, it was rated as more discredited than other therapies such as psychotherapy for the treatment of penis envy (which received a marginally lower, better score of 3.52). Even acupuncture for the treatment of mental and behavioural disorders received a more favourable (i.e. less discredited) rating of 3.49." If you're unsure, read his analysis at http://www.robyeung.com/why-should-you-be-wary-about-nlp/

Look, even if NLP worked, is it right to use a form of hypnosis in order to reel in your next customer? It's tempting to look for an easy fix, instead of learning to sell the right way. And Belfort is all about that easy fix.

Belfort also recommends salespeople study up on body language. But the problem is that, despite what you've heard, body language is more speculation than science. If you wish to read about how much to truly rely on body language, get the fascinating book "Spy the Lie," which was written by three CIA officers. They claim it's bad science, and they should know.

Belfort has a slavish devotion to scripts, which should only be applicable to green sales teams. If your salespeople are truly good, a script must be merely a starting point, because the best salespeople know how to sell already, and they've been proven to do it right.

Look: There is some good advice in Belfort's book, which is lifted from the materials of genuine sales and management experts. That advice can be easily acquired from less distasteful sources.

It's a huge mistake to assume that someone with an obvious

personality disorder should be emulated instead of avoided. Those who idolize Belfort are like a school bully's sidekicks. Don't be the school bully. And don't be a sidekick. Be principled enough to be a trailblazer and do the right thing, instead.

Since Belfort's management style is unprincipled, and he's been convicted of fraud, and (to the best of my knowledge) has still not paid back his debtors, perhaps he's not the best hero to uphold to your sales staff unless you, too, want to get into hot water. Which is, apparently, the way of the wolf.

BULLYING

Despite our attempts to stamp it out in the schools and on-line, it's thriving in the workplace. Why are so many people tempted to abuse salespeople, in particular? I think it's because there's a love/hate relationship dynamic.

Years ago when I was the Marketing Director for a custom homebuilder, I would watch the sales people come into the offices with great fanfare. "June" was larger than life. She had a loud voice, wore flashy clothes that were always the latest fashion, and had a laugh that echoed down the hallways. She was someone that caught your attention, and that made some people jealous.

I thought she was fabulous. I listened as people tore her apart behind her back. I'm ashamed I was too young then to have the courage to point out that she was the one who kept us all afloat.

Even company owners and sales managers seem to wobble between envy and resentment of their salespeople. Salespeople are the ones that do the work, take the chances, and only if and when it pays off do they get the fat paycheck. They are taking the risk that the owners and managers themselves won't usually take.

However, it's inevitable that salespeople are usually doomed from the beginning. They come in as rock stars and if they thrive, their rise is meteoric. But then the jealousy starts, and the tongues begin wagging.

Instead of seeing that salesperson as the hunter that is sent out on behalf of the tribe, the tribe begins to believe that they don't need the hunter.

Owners eventually tire of paying their salespeople more than most of the other employees. They hear the snarky stuff that is said about a particular salesperson, and they suddenly wonder if that salesperson might, perhaps, be overrated. Is she making too much money? If we shave off a percentage from her commission, she'll simply be motivated to sell more, right?

Let's say you're building a log cabin. You have a donkey that you use to haul lumber every day. One day you realize that you can load another log into the donkey's cart and, although she has to work a little harder, she gets it done. You do the same the next day. Then the next. Now she's hauling three more logs than she originally did.

Then you think that if you added yet *another* log to the cart, she could probably handle it. She's proven that she can haul an extra *three*, so why not four? However, this seems to be too much, and she's suddenly incapable of pulling the cart at all. If you start to flog her mercilessly, will she perform better?

"No!" you say, in horror. "She won't perform better and that's simply cruel!"

Ah, but how much crueler is it to push a human being past their limits? And yet I've seen this very thing done my entire life. Salespeople are brought in, and the work is gradually piled higher, and expectations become unreasonable. That's usually why sales teams come and go. And salespeople aren't all the same. If you get a good one, you need to keep her. And it starts with respect.

As I mentioned earlier, the tribe has a tendency to resent hunters. They see hunters as not entirely a part of the tribe, because hunters often disappear regularly to find the next big kill.

They're rarely part of group activities. This sense of "other" makes it easier for the tribe to give in to petty behaviors and jealousies. Whether we like it or not, bullying is part of human nature. There will always be bullies in the workplace. It's up to the company to decide if bullying should be tolerated.

"Of course bullying should never be tolerated!" you say. But I'll bet you also don't think it exists in your organization. Chances are that you're wrong. Often, the people at the top rarely hear what's really going on. Their subordinates are too busy telling them what they want to hear, instead.

In 2019, 94% of the people surveyed by Monster.com reported they were bullied at work. The percentage may have dropped slightly now that so many of us work from home. But, speaking from hard-won experience: The problem has not disappeared. If anything, it's hibernating.

You see, I've also been bullied at work. I chose to fight back. But fighting back is rarely successful, and everyone suffers.

If you're in charge, choose to open your eyes and unplug your ears. Don't tolerate workplace gossip. Discourage snarky put-downs. If there's a real problem, tell them to bring it to you directly, and mean it.

IF YOU'RE BEING BULLIED, THERE'S HELP

Standing up to a bully is hard, but living under his thumb is harder. Avoid it if you can. Here are some ways to check for red flags before you accept a job offer:

- Look over their Glassdoor reviews. In my case, the company that encouraged the bullying had very poor reviews (except for the ridiculously glowing ones obviously planted by their HR department).
- Look for similar reviews on Indeed and employment sites.

- Use LinkedIn to look up the people that work there. Do a search on the key players.
- Check out how they treat their customers by skimming through business reviews on Google, Yelp, and the Better Business Bureau. If they treat their clients badly, you'll be treated worse.

But if you're already in the situation, consider hiring a lawyer to represent you, or consult an HR expert, which is what I did.

Never forget that the company HR Department is not on your side, unless they're forced to be. They exist at the behest of your employer and will always put the company's needs ahead of your own. Document the issues by sending an email to yourself from your personal, not corporate, account. Emails are admissible in a court of law, and are also time and date stamped. When appropriate, continue to respectfully report each occurence to the company HR Department, unless it could place you in an even worse scenario.

Of course, you should immediately start looking for your next opportunity. Even if you're not their official spokesperson, you still are a de facto spokesperson for that company. As long as you remain there, you are presenting a false picture. If you can't honestly say that this is an employer you're proud to work for, get out. And if you see someone else being bullied, don't relax. Your turn is coming.

According to workplacebullying.org, "Abuse at work is the only form of abuse in America that is not yet taboo." And to everyone who is being bullied: You're not alone.

Resources I recommend include the book *Boundaries: When to Say YES, When to Say NO, To Take Control of Your Life* (Cloud/Townsend). Add your support for the Healthy Workplace Bill at healthyworkplacebill.org and get help and advice at WorkplaceBullying.org.

Finally, consider becoming an activist to end workplace

bullying, and please let me know if you do!

My happy outcome was choosing to create a company I could be proud of, where no bullying is tolerated under any circumstances. We are supportive of each other, and I never have to worry about what anyone on the team has to say about us. Therefore, we are getting free, positive publicity from every member of the team, along with their friends and family.

MICROMANAGEMENT vs. NECESSARY MANAGEMENT

Resist micromanaging your salespeople. The best hunters can't operate well in those circumstances. You can't go after big game if someone is constantly pulling you back or distracting you. On the other hand, managers need to know what their salespeople are doing, and it's best to see problems before they happen. This means you naturally want good communication and regular reporting. Yet, salespeople want to be left alone so that they can concentrate on the next big deal. What to do?

Decide what metrics you need, and what you can live without. Whatever metrics are *absolutely necessary* are the metrics you should demand. Then insist on an end-of-week report and stick to that. Some of the metrics that you need to know might be:

1. How many contacts were made this week?
2. How many sales?
3. How much were the sales?
4. What ongoing talks could result in sales?
   a What is the price expected from each deal?
   b When are the projected closing dates?
5. Where did the leads come from?

Other metrics might include data that is exclusive to your industry or your company. Again, salespeople are, by nature, not bean counters. You need to help them help you.

One way to make sure you get consistent information is if you tie it into the system in such a way that they must input the information in order to proceed. For example, they don't get paid until all of the completed paperwork has been turned in. Or perhaps you can arrange it so that they can't access the next customer until they put in the required information for the current customer.

Again, be aware that salespeople will look for ways to work around the system. As much as that might anger you, step back and take a deep breath. Remember that their goals are mostly in alignment with yours, but they rank sales higher than you sometimes will. For them, sales will always be the ultimate goal, and other stuff can sometimes just get in the way.

That being said, it must be restated that you can never excuse outright dishonesty. A salesperson who admits they did something wrong and tries to correct it is someone worth keeping. A salesperson who lies to get around what you are asking them to do is a liability.

MUSHROOMS

Sometimes salespeople are turned into mushrooms: Management keeps them in the dark, and feeds them crap. Salespeople are only as good as the information they're given. They must be up to date on all publicity and marketing efforts and need to know when changes happen, including anything from pricing to products.

Keeping this in mind, don't forget that salespeople are also often your best publicists. They are more powerful than you might realize. Happy salespeople demonstrate that you care about more than the bottom line. They represent you in the community. A good salesperson isn't a brainless machine who takes sales orders. Clerks take orders. Good salespeople make them.

Salespeople need to be regularly consulted about your

marketing efforts. What's working for them? What could be done better?

Tell them every time you or your company is mentioned in the media. Press coverage is golden material in sales. It's proof that the company is an expert in the field and not just a fly-by-night organization.

The feedback goes both ways. Salespeople talk to other employees and fellow salespeople, and they're out in the community. So, they're often more informed than management! Use that. Regularly ask them what's new.

Remember to bring your salespeople into your company-wide meetings so that they can listen and contribute. You don't have meetings that last more than ten minutes, do you? If you do, then it may be time to rethink those meetings, too. If you're ever in doubt, determine what you're spending in payroll per minute. That will motivate you to hurry everyone along.

Don't engage in something that can't be handled with a quick email. And don't force people to be in that meeting unless they're an integral part of it. My favorite solution comes from a company that forces everyone to stand during these meetings. It's amazing how quickly those meetings come to an end.

TEAM BUILDING

If possible, encourage everyone to participate in team-building events. That brings the tribe together and creates cohesiveness. It doesn't have to be some expensive outing to a mountain resort where you zipline down the mountain together. It can be an end of week potluck, a birthday party, a celebration of a sale. Make sure that your salespeople are a part of these events. If they're out in the field, tell them to be certain to be back on time for the get-together. It's for their own good, as well as yours.

Incidentally, these team-building events are always a publicity opportunity. Make sure pictures are posted on all your social media platforms. Your clients like to know that you treat your employees well, and potential employees will be impressed by how you treat your staff. This means you will get to choose employees from a better pool of talent, instead of settling for the guy that was too stupid to read your Glassdoor reviews.

Be careful to not show favoritism in public. Some owners or managers are so delighted by their salespeople that they'll praise them loudly to everyone in hearing range. That's great, as long as you do the same thing for your administrative assistant, your accountant, and your receptionist. A lack of obvious favoritism goes a long way toward reinforcing the team mentality. Yes, praise in public and scold in private. But do all things in moderation, or you could inadvertently be placing a target on your favorite's back.

DON'T ENCOURAGE DESPERATION

Don't pay your salespeople peanuts in the hopes that a fat commission will entice them to do their job. Instead, pay them well, add a commission on top of that, and expect the best from them. Salespeople have families, just like you do, and need a steady paycheck they can rely on. Think of commissions as the icing on the cake.

You see, a good salesperson will be building a pipeline, as well as pitching and closing sales. You must invest in them, so that they can invest in you. If the salesperson doesn't perform according to reasonable expectations, say goodbye and find one that can.

Also, I don't recommend SPIFs (Sales Program Incentive Funds). SPIFs are management's way of encouraging salespeople to go over the top and reach for that one last sale that could be hanging out there. A SPIF could be two tickets to the movies for that week's highest producer, or a $100 bonus if that salesperson is able to sell one more widget. But just like the parable of The Tortoise and the Hare: Slow and steady wins the race. Instead of SPIFs, pay them well and keep them accountable.

SPIFs encourage desperate behavior.

Let's face it: If a salesperson is good, they are good. They should be expected to do their job well. But, salespeople are no different than anyone else. They like and need money - the more, the better. If you give them a SPIF with the hopes that they'll try harder, it is a good bet that they really can't do better than they usually do. Instead, they'll cut corners, make deals they shouldn't, or take unwise chances so that they can get that extra bonus.

I once worked for a company that told me, "Hey, when you go to that conference, we'll give you a $1000 bonus if you can get more than X number of customers." I asked if I was allowed to make deals, and they said I could (within a limit). I made those deals, within that limit. But, ultimately they were very unhappy with the overall revenue loss and resented paying me the $1000 bonus, even though I'd earned it. The moral of this story is: Be careful what you ask for.

SALESPEOPLE THRIVE WITH OTHER SALESPEOPLE

Salespeople are generally extroverts who need to be around other people. Locking them in an office or, even worse, in a cubicle by themselves can be counterproductive. Salespeople do need privacy just like anyone else (especially if they're on the phone), but allow them to mix with each other and learn tactics on company time.

I don't mean that they should be allowed to stand in the halls and talk with each other all day. I mean that there should be a sales meeting each week where they talk with each other about problems and victories that they encountered that week. Often if sales managers or owners stay quiet, they'll learn more than if they try to guide the conversation. When something works, it may work for everyone! That's important information. And if one salesperson has hit a hard stop and can't get past it, another salesperson may solve not only his problem, but the problem that everyone else has had.

If you only have one salesperson (or if you are your own salesperson), look into sales groups outside of your company that might offer support and advice.

AVOID 1099 SALESPEOPLE

A 1099 is the tax form an independent contractor fills out when they choose to work with a firm. These independent contractors are just that: independent. And don't you forget it.

There seem to be two types of companies that hire 1099 salespeople. Fly-by-night companies, and companies with no money. And there is only one type of salesperson that is okay being an independent contractor: desperate.

There are rare exceptions. For instance, you may have a start-up company and a truly fantastic product, but you simply don't have the money to hire someone. You advertise for an independent salesperson and maybe you'll get lucky. And maybe you won't.

You'll also grow frustrated by the lack of control you have over this salesperson. By law, you cannot tell them what hours they must work. You'll only be paying them for the sales they make because, traditionally, these salespeople are paid "commission only." This means they will have no vested interest in you or your firm's image or corporate culture. Good salespeople are hunters who hunt for the tribe. 1099 sales people only hunt for themselves, and this ultimately never works well.

And if you're someone considering taking a 1099 position, think about it twice. Traditionally these companies have high turnover rates. If they don't believe enough in their own product to invest in salespeople, why should you believe in it enough to work for free until, and if, you sell that product?

Reputable salespeople avoid these situations.

SELLING IN AN ONLINE WORLD

COVID-19 changed the way we live and work, so it's no surprise that sales roles have also changed. At the same time, the government continues to tighten regulations on telephone solicitors. And, let's face it, we all hate those telemarketing calls.

But now your salespeople can't always drop in on clients, or potential clients, unannounced. In fact, many businesses have sold or rented out their former offices. Telework has finally reached widespread acceptance.

Even if we finally conquer COVID-19 and all its variants, we still have seen a major shift to online business. These days, if you want to see someone face-to-face, you set up a meeting on Zoom or Google Meet.

So, how can potential clients and customers be reached?

Well, it's still possible for your salespeople to call potential clients. But make sure that you know both your state and federal regulations so that you understand what parameters they can operate in. Salespeople who are calling a lead may appear to be telemarketing even if that's not their intention.

But, what works best in a post COVID-19 world is social selling.

89% of top performing salespeople say that social networks are important in closing deals. 70% of them use LinkedIn for business, 64% use Facebook, and 43% use Twitter. 64% of salespeople that choose to hunt with social media hit their team quota. Salespeople that don't use it will only hit their goals 49% of the time. The top social sellers manage to create 45% more sales opportunities than their peers, according to LinkedIn and Superoffice.com.

Over 75% of buyers use the internet to make purchasing decisions, so this is logical. Embrace this. Offer to cover your salespeople's LinkedIn Premium account. Introduce your social media team as advisors to the sales team. When a publicity win happens, have your social media team post it across all platforms, and then either tag your salespeople or have the social media team send them a link, so your salespeople can repost it if they choose. Keep them current with any marketing campaigns and special offers.

Another way to enhance your salespeople's abilities: Offer training that will result in certifications. A large majority of all buyers are willing to engage in discussions if they're with an industry expert.

There are some companies that will doubtless be alarmed by the thought of their salespeople active in such public forums. Certainly, micromanagers will be running themselves ragged trying to monitor what their employees are doing. That's why it's more important than ever to carefully choose the salespeople that will be your representatives and always keep them well-informed.

SALES TECHNIQUES THAT WORK FOR ONE COMPANY MIGHT NOT WORK IN ANOTHER ENVIRONMENT

Perhaps some of the disdain people feel for salespeople comes from the notorious used car salesman archetype, and obviously Jordan Belfort (mentioned earlier) contributes to some of that.

The good news is that there is room in this world for all types of salespeople. You need to ask what type you want to represent you because, remember, they are your ambassadors. When people think of you and your company, your salesperson will usually be the first person the clients think about.

Some salespeople will be a great fit for your environment. Some won't. Environments vary, and so do sales tactics.

When I worked for the MFRM product lines (Mattress Firm / Furniture Firm / Aqua Firm) I was a national events and expositions specialist. I was expected to be at my best at all times *(no pressure or anything)*. I was always among the top 60 (and often in the top 30) employees in the entire company (of over 30,000 employees at that time) and I'm still proud of that.

Overall, my selling style has always been "relational," which means that I build genuine relationships over a period of time with clients, because I truly care about them. Although I can't sell something I don't believe in, if I feel that my product is the right product for the client, chances are excellent that they'll be buying it from me!

When I was working for the MFRM brands, I absolutely believed in the products that I sold. But, we flew all over the country, selling high-end beds, spas, and massage chairs at major events. There was no time to build relationships with customers and no time for fear. If relationship sales are an elegant classical music concert, this type of selling was a straight up mosh pit. But it worked, and it was exhilarating!

The most effective representatives moved fast. They were able to quickly entice someone to try the product. This involved getting the potential client on a mattress, stepping into a dry spa, or sitting in a massage chair. The customers were able to experience the product, while the representative showed them all the features. Once the customer decided that they loved the mattress, chair, or spa, the price was the next objective to overcome through a variety of fast responses and quick negotiations. After that, the only thing left was the payment and delivery arrangements.

Yes, a small portion of this was still relationship building. After all, a customer must always like you if they're going to trust you and make a purchase. However, the majority of the techniques were built from a variety of sources and weren't based on anything more than a rudimentary connection. Some of these sources were books that were mandatory reading for the entire team (I'll share a few of these books with you later) and some sources were the team leaders, who had perfected these techniques over time.

The team leaders made it quite clear that the team structure was very similar to the military. And, like the military, many of us forged bonds that still last many years later. I would drop anything to help some of them to this day. It was a band of brothers (with an occasional sister).

Also like the military, they ran a tight ship. There were high expectations, and everyone had to always be at peak performance. We were "on" the moment the doors opened, and remained "on" sometimes for twelve hours or more. But even when they demanded a lot, they also gave a lot. They paid us well, they put us up in the best hotels, gave us a generous food allowance, and often our team was a family substitute when we needed it.

I loved my time with them, and was about to be promoted when I chose to step down to help out my aging parents, who needed me more.

But as much as I enjoyed that time, I don't believe those sales techniques could be (or even should be) reproduced in most environments. Those tactics were developed for a particular type of product in a particular type of setting with a particular type of customer.

Not all selling techniques will be a good fit for every type of business. If your best chance of selling a car is the first time a client sets foot in your car lot, then a more aggressive selling style may be your best option.

There are some car dealerships that actually test potential salespeople for psychopathic traits. If the salesperson tests out as a mild psychopath (there are levels of psychopathy) then the dealership will hire them. These dealerships know that they want sales and they don't care if some grandma is sold a lemon. Other dealerships feel that the risk of negative publicity is too great.

If you're not sure what type of techniques you or your

salespeople should be using, read some of the books I recommend below. Look at your competition and see what works for them. Consider calling in an expert. It's best to be cautious when taking advice from close friends or family members, and be careful with your employees. No matter how much you like them, they have their own hidden agendas and their own weak spots. Get their feedback, but weigh it along with everyone else's.

When you've decided what type of sales team will best represent your company, you can then build a strong team. Take the time to put together a list of what traits you definitely want in your salespeople, and what traits you definitely don't want.

No matter what: Never forget that your salesperson is your representative.

STAYING ON TOP OF TRENDS THE EASY WAY

Now that you've reached the end of the book, you may be frustrated. It's obvious that there's a lot to understand, and trends and practices are always changing. "How can I stay on top of everything?" you ask.

You can enrich your business and yourself by encouraging your employees, including your salespeople, to do the research for you.

Give everyone a book allowance. If they want to buy a book in their field, have them submit a request to you. As long as you agree it's a valuable book that will help them be better employees, buy it for them and ask them to write you a summary of the book when they're finished. This means your salespeople will keep you informed about the latest sales trends, and your marketing department should keep you abreast of the newest marketing data and publicity ideas.

If you see a book you think they should read, buy it for them as a bonus (but take them out for coffee so you can also learn from it).

If you have a company-wide folder where everyone shares summaries of the latest books, everyone in the company can be kept in the loop. In that folder, keep a sub-folder with your marketing campaigns and publicity wins. This is information that anyone in the company can learn from.

Consider having a monthly chat session where everyone talks about something important that they discovered. Remember that an educated employee who is thriving is often the best publicity you can have.

RECOMMENDED SALES AND MANAGEMENT READING

When I taught the graduate level Management Skills course at the University of South Florida (under Dr. Jay Knippen), we loaded our students down with huge amounts of reading material. Over time, the business world showed me what was truly effective and what was more of a philosophical pipe dream.

Therefore, instead of suggesting the latest fad books or the supposed classics, I'm going to give you a list of what I feel to be effective books that are truly useful. Some of these books are on leadership, some on selling. But all are worth reading, whether you're in management or sales.

Go for No! Yes is the Destination, No is How You Get There (Fenton/Waltz)

Hug Your Haters: How to Embrace Complaints and Keep Your Customers (Baer). Although I don't always agree with Baer's methods, this book is a solid piece of research and worth reading.

Pitch Like a Girl: How a Woman Can Be Herself and Still Succeed (Lichtenberg)

The Art of Closing the Sale (Tracy)

The 21 Irrefutable Laws of Leadership: Follow Them and People Will Follow You (Maxwell)

Wooden on Leadership: How to Create a Winning Organization (Wooden/Jamison). If you're undecided about this one, look for my review on LinkedIn.

AFTERWORD

My mother, Karen Y. Davis, was an author. It's a shame she passed away unexpectedly in 2020, and will never get the chance to see this book. I think she'd love it. She was the one who inadvertently introduced me to the magic of publicity and marketing.

One day when I was young and bored, I found an old copy of *The Hidden Persuaders*, by Vance Packard. Mom had read the 1964 edition, shelved it, and forgotten about it. Years later, I picked it up and was immediately entranced.

Ironically, Packard was a critic of consumerism. He felt that the public was being manipulated by slick marketers, and he was determined to pull back the curtain and reveal The Great Oz. Many marketers and publicists took offense, claiming it was sensationalized and designed to create a scandal. No doubt, it was.

Over time, many of Packard's accusations have been proven to be unfounded. Yet what I adored was seeing how marketing and publicity were able to reframe mistaken impressions and help consumers discover new experiences.

One of Packard's tales made a big impression on me. Prunes had become associated with laxatives to the extent that people weren't buying them. So, the California Prune Advisory Board turned to the Institute for Motivational Research. A fresh marketing tactic was developed: Prunes would be touted as delicious, with pictures of happy people enjoying them, and they were even showcased in desserts. Sales skyrocketed.

After I read this case study, I begged Mom to buy prunes so that I could try them out. Sure enough, I found that they were far more delicious than those little dry raisins that were tucked in our lunchboxes. And yes, I also discovered that they had to be sampled in moderation.

I'm opposed to manipulation. But, I believe that effective marketing is not necessarily unethical. Instead, if publicity and marketing campaigns are properly crafted, they can educate the public on what is available, and why they should love it every bit as much as you do. They can capture attention, and create excitement. They can convey your message powerfully, allowing you to be heard in places far beyond your local market. They can level the playing field.

I hope that I effectively showed you how you can put your publicity campaign on steroids. If you have any questions or comments, or if I can help you in any way, please feel free to contact me. You can reach me and my team, The Reps, at thereps.net.

I've also teamed up with Alive Executive Publishing, where I'm part of a powerhouse that will not only publish and market your book, we'll also publicize it! You can find us at aliveexecutivepublishing.com.

If you want to talk with me, get in touch with me now, before you get distracted by life. I'm looking forward to hearing about you and your latest, exciting project!

About The Author

Frēda has vast experience in public relations and marketing. She appears regularly on radio and television, and teaches marketing and publicity techniques at group seminars and other events.

Frēda hosted *The Business Edge* radio show and was a regular guest and fill-in host on many other radio shows. She is considered a thought leader by her peers and is an accomplished author and editor, having contributed to various publications in a variety of fields. Frēda was featured in "One Word That Will Change Your Life" (2020) and "Credibility Nation" (2020). She has received numerous awards, including The 2018 Spotlight Award by Dustin Burleson Seminars for her "service and contribution ... and unparalleled coaching to doctors and their employees."

She has always been active in her community, serving on many boards and in other capacities, and believes the only wasted life is the life without learning.

ABOOKS

ALIVE Book Publishing and ALIVE Publishing Group
are imprints of Advanced Publishing LLC,
3200 A Danville Blvd., Suite 204, Alamo, California 94507

Telephone: 925.837.7303
alivebookpublishing.com

www.ingramcontent.com/pod-product-compliance
Lightning Source LLC
Chambersburg PA
CBHW031935190326
41519CB00007B/548